TruResilience Workbook:

The Proven Path to Reprogramming Your Mind and Reclaiming Your Future

A Hands-on Daily Strategies Guide to Rebuild, Reinvent, and Rise Above Your Past

Jackie Truman

TruAlchemy Productions Inc.

Table of Contents

Introduction

This Workbook Is Your Roadmap Home

You've made it to this moment—standing at the edge of the life you've always wanted.

If you're holding this workbook, chances are you've already taken the first courageous step: cracking open the pages of *TruResilience* and deciding that, yeah, maybe your story isn't finished after all.

Maybe you've felt the sting of doors slammed in your face because of a past that just won't stay buried. Maybe you've carried the weight of labels like a ball and chain, wondering if you'll ever truly be seen for who you are, not who you were. Or maybe you simply woke up one day and realized you were tired of feeling like a passenger in your own life.

I get it. I've been there. This workbook isn't about wishful thinking—it's about taking control, building real change, and never going back to the life that held you down. Think of it as your travel companion for navigating the path toward rewriting your story. This is for those of us who know what it feels like to be seen as a "lost cause," as if your history dictates your destiny.

If *TruResilience* is the map, consider this workbook your compass, journal, and toolbox all rolled into one. It's designed to help you move beyond simply reading about change and to start living it.

Why This Workbook Matters

Look, there are a million self-help books out there promising overnight transformations. But let's be real: you didn't pick up *TruResilience* because you were looking for a quick fix. You picked it up because you're ready to do the real work – the kind that digs deep, confronts the shadows, and builds a foundation of resilience that can withstand anything life throws your way.

The world doesn't always make it easy for those of us with a past to disclose. The beauty of this workbook is that it allows you to move beyond reading a story of resilience and start creating your own personal legacy.

This workbook isn't about slapping a coat of positivity over deep wounds. It's about getting your hands dirty, facing those wounds head-on, and using them as fuel to build something stronger. It's about acknowledging where you've been, accepting where you are, and taking deliberate steps toward where you want to be.

How to Use This Workbook

This isn't a race. There's no "right" or "wrong" way to work through these pages. Think of it as a conversation with yourself – a safe space to explore your thoughts, challenge your beliefs, and track your progress.

A Few Guiding Principles:

- **Be brutally honest:** This workbook is for your eyes only (and maybe your therapist). The more honest you are with yourself, the more you'll get out of it. Don't sugarcoat your struggles; instead, dive right into them!

- **Start where you are:** Don't feel pressured to start on page one and work your way through in a linear fashion. Jump around! Focus on the exercises that resonate with you in the moment. This process should feel empowering, not overwhelming.

- **Embrace the mess:** Transformation is messy. There will be moments of clarity, moments of confusion, and moments when you just want to throw the whole thing in the trash. That's okay. Stick with it.

- **Track your wins (and your stumbles):** The progress trackers in this workbook are designed to help you see how far you've come, even when it doesn't feel like you're moving forward. Celebrate the small victories, and don't beat yourself up over the setbacks.

- **Adapt the exercises to your story:** Every exercise can be adapted to where you are right now, and where you're headed. Use these prompts as launching points!

- **Remember, small is sustainable:** Think of your change as the steady flow of a river versus a rushing flash flood.

A Few Things to Keep in Mind:

- You are not alone. If you find yourself struggling with any of the exercises, remember that there are resources available to help. Reach out to a trusted friend, mentor, or therapist.

- Your story matters. Every experience you've had, every obstacle you've overcome, has shaped you into the person you are today. This workbook is a celebration of that journey.

- It's not all at once, or nothing. The beauty of change is that it happens in the margins of your life. Don't feel like you have to take on every challenge. Just the smallest, sustained actions are what will carry you to where you need to be!

Before We Dive In

Take a few moments to complete the *Self-Assessment Quiz* on the next page. This will give you a snapshot of where you're starting from and help you identify areas where you want to focus your energy. Then, write a *Letter to Your Future Self* – a message of intention, hope, and commitment to the journey ahead.

This is more than just a workbook; it's a declaration that you are ready to rewrite your story and reclaim your power.

So, grab a pen, take a deep breath, and let's get started with some pre-work.

Your new life begins now.

Self-Assessment Quiz

Where Are You Starting From?

This quiz is designed to provide a snapshot of your current mindset, habits, and environment. Answer honestly – there are no right or wrong answers! Circle the number that best reflects your current reality.

Scoring:

- 1 = Strongly Disagree
- 2 = Disagree
- 3 = Neutral
- 4 = Agree
- 5 = Strongly Agree

Mindset & Beliefs

1. I often feel trapped by my past mistakes. 1 2 3 4 5

2. I believe I have the power to change my life, regardless of my circumstances. 1 2 3 4 5

3. I tend to focus on my limitations rather than my strengths. 1 2 3 4 5

4. I view challenges as opportunities for growth. 1 2 3 4 5

5. I am worthy of success and happiness. 1 2 3 4 5

6. I often compare myself to others, leading to feelings of inadequacy. 1 2 3 4 5

7. I trust my instincts and decision-making abilities. 1 2 3 4 5

8. I struggle with negative self-talk and self-criticism. 1 2 3 4 5

Habits & Behaviors

9. I consistently work towards my goals, even when faced with setbacks. 1 2 3 4 5

10. I have a clear understanding of my values and live in alignment with them. 1 2 3 4 5

11. I prioritize self-care and well-being in my daily routine. 1 2 3 4 5

12. I struggle with procrastination and lack of self-discipline. 1 2 3 4 5

13. I actively seek out new learning opportunities and challenges. 1 2 3 4 5

14. I am comfortable setting boundaries and saying no to others when necessary. 1 2 3 4 5

15. I regularly engage in activities that bring me joy and fulfillment. 1 2 3 4 5

16. I find it difficult to break free from old, destructive patterns. 1 2 3 4 5

Environment & Relationships

17. I feel supported and encouraged by the people in my life. 1 2 3 4 5

18. I have healthy boundaries in my relationships. 1 2 3 4 5

19. I am surrounded by positive and growth-oriented influences. 1 2 3 4 5

20. I often feel drained or negatively impacted by certain people or environments. 1 2 3 4 5

21. I actively cultivate meaningful connections with others. 1 2 3 4 5

22. I am able to effectively navigate challenging or toxic relationships. 1 2 3 4 5

23. My environment promotes personal growth and well-being. 1 2 3 4 5

24. I often feel isolated or unsupported in my journey. 1 2 3 4 5

Scoring & Interpretation

- **Total Score for Mindset & Beliefs (Questions 1-8):** ....
- **Total Score for Habits & Behaviors (Questions 9-16):** ....
- **Total Score for Environment & Relationships (Questions 17-24):** ....

Interpreting Your Scores:

- **1-20 in any category:** Indicates significant challenges and areas for growth. Focus on the corresponding chapters in this workbook.

- **21-30 in any category:** Suggests some progress but also areas where focused effort can lead to substantial improvements.

- **31-40 in any category:** Reflects a solid foundation and positive patterns. Continue reinforcing these strengths and exploring further growth.

Notes: Use this space to jot down any immediate thoughts or insights that came up while taking the quiz. What areas do you feel most drawn to working on first?

This self-assessment provides a starting point. Throughout your journey with this workbook, revisit this quiz periodically to track your progress and celebrate your growth!

Knowledge is power!

Letter to My Future Self:

A Promise of Resilience

Throughout this journey of rebuilding your life, you'll confront powerful emotions, uncover deep truths, and reclaim the strength that may have been hidden beneath layers of hardship. Writing a letter to your future self is a powerful act—an opportunity to envision your life transformed by resilience, clarity, and purpose. This isn't simply an exercise in imagination; it's an act of intention, a declaration of your commitment to breaking free from old cycles.

Below is a sample letter inspired by my own journey. As you read it, think about what you deeply desire for yourself in the next 30 days and beyond. Allow this to inspire your own words, knowing your future self awaits the encouragement, strength, and compassion only you can provide. (Space at back of this workbook.)

Sample Letter to My Future Self

Dear Future Me,

I'm writing this letter today because I know you're reading it from a place I can only dream about right now—a place of clarity, freedom, and authentic joy. Today, things feel tough. The old cycles still pull at me, and sometimes the weight of the past feels heavier than I'd like to admit. But here's the thing: today, I'm deciding to break that cycle. I'm choosing differently.

I promise to show up for you every day. I promise to confront my fears, question my limiting beliefs, and actively rewrite the story I tell myself about who I am and what I'm capable of. I'm committing to self-compassion, discipline, and courage—even when it feels impossible. And when setbacks happen (because they will), I'll remind myself that setbacks don't define my journey; resilience does.

By the time you're reading this, I know you'll have made remarkable strides forward. You'll have replaced old habits with healthier, empowering ones. You'll have embraced your worth and reclaimed your voice. You'll see yourself not as someone defined by trauma or setbacks, but as someone shaped by courage, strength, and unwavering hope.

I'm proud of you already. Keep going.

With compassion and faith,

-Jackie

Commitment Contract:

My Promise to Myself

Welcome to the beginning of your transformation.

This workbook is not just a set of exercises—it's a blueprint for breaking cycles, reclaiming your life, and creating a future that once seemed impossible.

But transformation isn't automatic. It requires commitment, action, and a decision to **never go back to the version of yourself that accepted less than you deserve.**

By signing this contract, you are making a **personal commitment** to yourself. **You are not promising perfection—you are promising persistence.**

This is your declaration that, from this moment on, you are moving forward.

My Transformation Commitment

I, _____, declare that I am no longer a prisoner of my past.

I commit to:

- **Breaking free from negative cycles** and refusing to be defined by my mistakes.
- **Taking full responsibility** for my growth, choices, and future.
- **Embracing discipline and resilience** even when the journey gets tough.
- **Holding myself accountable** to the goals I set and the man I am becoming.
- **Continuing to learn, grow, and push beyond my comfort zone.**
- **Surrounding myself with people and habits that support my success.**
- **Staying true to my vision and refusing to quit on myself.**

I understand that real change happens one decision, **one action, and one day at a time.**

I commit to showing up for myself, to following through, and to making my future something I am proud of.

Today, I choose my transformation. **No more excuses. No more looking back.**

Signature: _____

Date: _____

Chapter 1

Breaking the Cycle

Welcome to the first deep dive in reclaiming your story.

This chapter isn't about pointing fingers or dwelling on past mistakes. It's about shining a light on the unseen forces that have been quietly dictating your choices and steering you off course. We're going to dig deep, expose hidden beliefs, and give you the tools to reset your mindset and start moving toward the life you deserve. The next thirty days are designed to help you understand how these negative patterns, if they exist, have impacted who you have become. **Are you tired of repeating the same story everyone else wrote for you? Time to take it back, it's yours!**

At 18, Jay Jordan's life changed forever when he was arrested for vehicle theft and sentenced to seven years in prison. Like so many others who enter the system, he believed that his past mistakes had sealed his fate. Society had already decided who he was—a convicted felon, a lost cause.

But Jay refused to accept that narrative. While incarcerated, he made a critical decision: to challenge the beliefs that had kept him trapped in the same cycles of failure. He **studied, reflected, and committed himself to personal transformation.** He realized that true freedom wasn't just about getting out of prison—**it was about breaking free from the mindset that had led him there in the first place.**

After his release, Jay faced countless barriers. His record followed him, shutting him out of job opportunities, housing, and even the right to fully participate in society. But instead of giving up, he turned his struggles into **fuel for change.** Today, he is a powerful advocate for criminal justice reform and serves as the CEO of the Alliance for Safety and Justice, helping to create policies that remove barriers for formerly incarcerated individuals. Jay's story isn't just about beating the odds—it's about rewriting them entirely. His journey shows that **real transformation starts in the mind.** No matter where you've been or what you've done, change is possible.

Throughout this chapter, you'll begin the same process Jay did—identifying the hidden mental scripts that have kept you stuck and taking the first steps toward rewriting your story.

Week 1: Uncovering Hidden Scripts (Section 1.1)

Weekly Focus:

This week, you'll learn to recognize the hidden beliefs—those subconscious scripts—that have kept you trapped in negative patterns. By clearly seeing these patterns, you begin reclaiming your power to break free.

Day 1: Seeing Your Patterns Clearly

- **Today's Reflection Prompt:**

  "What negative thought, belief, or habit keeps showing up in my life?
  Why does it feel so difficult to break this cycle?"

  ....

  ....

  ..

- **Today's Affirmation:**

  "Today, I'm brave enough to face the patterns that have held me back."

- **Mini-Challenge (Small Win):**

  Notice and gently acknowledge one moment today where you fall into an old negative pattern. Jot it down here:

- **Reflection Check-in:** (Circle one number)

  How difficult was it to face this pattern today?
  Easy [1 – 2 – 3 – 4 – 5] Difficult

- **Daily Reflection Journal**

  - **Insight Check-in:**

    What insight or realization did I have today after completing this exercise?

  - **Meditation Moment (2–3 min):**

    Pause and breathe.

    Repeat quietly: "I am open to seeing clearly."

    ☐ Completed Meditation

Day 1 Tracker:

Activity	Completed?
Daily Reflection Journal	☐ Yes ☐ No
Affirmation Recited	☐ Yes ☐ No
Mini-Challenge Completed?	☐ Yes ☐ No

Day 2: Discovering Your Roots

- **Today's Reflection Prompt:**

  "When and where did this negative belief or habit first appear in my life?
  What experiences reinforced it over time?"

....

....

- **Today's Affirmation**

  "I have the strength to understand where my beliefs come from, without judgment."

- **Mini-Challenge:**

  Briefly write about the earliest memory associated with this negative belief:

....

....

My earliest memory connected to this belief is:

- **Daily Meditation:**

  (Visualize yourself letting go of one painful memory associated with this belief.)

- **Reflection Tracker:**

  How emotionally challenging was today's prompt?
  [1 (Easy) — 5 (Difficult)] _____

Day 3: Understanding the Emotional Cost

- **Today's Reflection Prompt:**

  "How has this negative pattern impacted my relationships, opportunities, or emotional well-being?"

....

....

- **Today's Affirmation:**
  "I recognize the cost of this belief and choose to release it."

- **Mini-Challenge:**
  Notice one specific moment today where your negative belief affected your choices. Write briefly about it here:

....

....

- **Meditation Check-In (2 min):**
  Breathe deeply. Remind yourself: "I am deserving of a new story."

Day 4: Identifying the Hidden Benefit

- **Today's Reflection Prompt:**
  "What has holding onto this negative belief protected me from?
  How might letting go of it be uncomfortable or challenging?"

....

....

- **Today's Affirmation:**
  "I acknowledge that change is uncomfortable, but I choose growth over familiarity."

- **Mini-Challenge:**
  Do one small thing today that challenges this old belief. (e.g., asking for help, applying for a job, calling a supportive person.)

- **Daily Check-in:**
  What feelings came up as I challenged myself today?

....

....

Day 5: Creating Empowering Beliefs

- **Today's Reflection Prompt:**
  "What positive belief or mindset could replace my negative script?"

....

....

- **Today's Affirmation:**
  "I have the power to create new empowering beliefs."

- **Action Step:**
  Write your new empowering belief clearly here. Say it aloud three times today:

....

- **My new empowering belief:** ....
  ....

  - **Meditation Moment:**
    (Imagine fully embodying this new belief, noticing how it feels.)

  - **Habit Tracker (Mark today's progress):**
    | Affirmation Recited ☐ | New Action Taken ☐ | Journal Reflection ☐ |

Day 6: Celebrating Weekly Progress & Reflection

- **Today's Reflection Prompt (Weekly Check-In):**
  "After working through this week's reflections, what clarity have I gained about the subconscious beliefs driving my cycles?"

....

....

- **Today's Affirmation:**
  "Every insight moves me closer to freedom."

- **Milestone Celebration:**
  Write down one powerful realization or breakthrough from this week:

- **Community Connection:**
  (Optional but recommended) Reach out to a trusted friend or accountability partner and share this week's realization.

Week 1 Summary:

- **Most helpful reflection this week:**

....

....

....

....

- **Biggest challenge:**

....

....

....

....

- **What's one way I noticed growth?**

....

....

....

....

Preparing for Next Week:

As we move forward, you'll start recognizing emotional traps and begin rewriting subconscious beliefs. Keep your workbook nearby, stay consistent, and remember:

You're not alone. Your future is yours to reclaim, one small step at a time.

Week 2: The Science of Breaking Free from Self-Sabotage (Section 1.2)

Weekly Focus:

This week, you'll explore how neuroscience can help you break the destructive cycle of self-sabotage. You'll learn practical strategies grounded in brain science, so you can actively replace negative patterns with habits that support your goals.

Remember:

Neuroscience proves your brain is capable of change (neuroplasticity). No matter how deeply ingrained your habits may feel, every thought, belief, and action is something you can rewrite.

Day 7: Recognizing Your Self-Sabotage Patterns

- **Today's Reflection Prompt:**
  "What are some ways I typically sabotage my progress or success? (e.g., procrastination, giving up easily, negative self-talk, avoidance)"

  ....

  ....

- **Today's Affirmation:**
  "I am honest with myself about patterns that no longer serve me."

- **Mini-Challenge:**
  Identify one moment today when you notice a self-sabotaging behavior arise. Write it down and briefly describe what triggered it.

  ....

  ....

- **Daily Tracker:**
  | Affirmation Recited ☐ | Self-Sabotage Recognized ☐ | Journal Completed ☐ |

- **Meditation Moment (2–3 min):**
  Breathe deeply. Affirm: "I am capable of changing my patterns."
  ☐ Completed Meditation

Day 8: Understanding How Your Brain Works

- **Today's Reflection Prompt:**

  "Reflecting on the concept of neuroplasticity—your brain's ability to change—which specific habit or pattern do you want to change the most?"

....

....

- **Today's Affirmation:**

  "My brain can learn new, healthier patterns."

- **Mini-Challenge:**

  Write down clearly one negative habit you want to replace and what positive habit you'll replace it with.

    - **Negative Habit:** _____

    - **Positive Replacement:** _____

- **Daily Check-in:**

  How motivated do you feel about making this change today?

  [Low 1 – 2 – 3 – 4 – 5 High]

Day 9: Rewiring Your Brain – Small Steps Count

- **Today's Reflection Prompt:**

  "What small daily action can I take consistently to build a healthier habit and rewire my brain over time?"

....

....

- **Today's Affirmation:**

  "Small, consistent actions lead to lasting change."

- **Mini-Challenge:**

  Perform one small action today aligned with the positive habit you identified yesterday.

- **Meditation Moment:**

(Visualize clearly what it feels like to successfully replace your old habit.)

Day 10: Learning from Your Patterns

- **Today's Reflection Prompt:**

"What benefit or comfort does my self-sabotaging behavior temporarily offer me? How can I fulfill that need in a healthier way?"

....

....

- **Today's Affirmation:**

"I meet my needs in ways that empower me rather than sabotage me."

- **Mini-Challenge:**

Choose one healthy, alternative action today when tempted by an old sabotaging behavior. Write about your experience:

....

....

- **Daily Tracker:**

| Affirmation Recited ☐ | Alternative Action Taken ☐ | Journal Completed ☐ |

Day 11: Creating Positive Neuro-pathways

- **Today's Reflection Prompt:**

"What positive feelings or outcomes can I reinforce when I successfully resist a self-sabotaging urge?"

....

....

- **Today's Affirmation:**

"Each positive choice strengthens my new pathways."

- **Action Step:**

Clearly write one positive affirmation or reward you can give yourself each time you successfully avoid self-sabotage:

....

- • **My Reward or Affirmation:**
  - • **Meditation Moment (2 min):**
    (Visualize reinforcing your positive choice and feel the pride and empowerment.)

Day 12: Weekly Reflection & Milestone Celebration

- • **Today's Reflection Prompt:**
  "What have I learned this week about how self-sabotage works, and what steps have I taken to begin changing these patterns?"

....

....

- • **Today's Affirmation:**
  "I am actively rewriting my future."

- • **Milestone Celebration:**
  Note one significant moment or insight this week that showed you clearly your capacity for change:

....

....

- • **My Milestone:**
  - • **Community Connection (Optional but Encouraged):**
    Share this week's milestone or insight with a trusted friend or support partner.

Week 2 Summary:

- • **Main self-sabotaging pattern I recognized:**

....

....

....

....

- **New strategy I learned to replace sabotage:**

....

....

....

....

- **My commitment for continued progress:**

....

....

....

....

Preparing for Next Week:

Next, we'll explore emotional traps that keep you stuck. You'll learn how deeply rooted emotions fuel self-sabotage and how you can overcome them to reclaim your power.

"You are stronger than your patterns—your future belongs to you."

Week 3: Emotional Traps Keeping You Stuck (Section 1.3)

Weekly Focus:

This week, you'll clearly identify the emotional traps—such as fear, guilt, shame, or anger—that keep you stuck in negative cycles. By understanding and facing these emotions directly, you can begin releasing their hold over your life.

Remember:

Jay Jordan learned that facing his fear and shame was crucial to moving forward. Your emotions don't define you—they inform you. Recognizing them is your first step toward freedom.

Day 13: Identifying Your Primary Emotional Trap

- **Today's Reflection Prompt:**

"Which emotion most frequently traps me or makes me feel stuck (e.g., fear, shame, anger, guilt)? How does it typically show up in my daily life?"

....

....

- **Today's Affirmation:**

"I am brave enough to acknowledge my emotions honestly."

- **Mini-Challenge:**

Notice and briefly document one specific moment today when this emotion was particularly strong.

- **Daily Tracker:**

| Affirmation Recited ☐ | Emotion Clearly Identified ☐ | Journal Completed ☐ |

- **Meditation Moment (2–3 min):**

Breathe deeply and remind yourself: "My emotions guide me—they do not control me."
☐ Completed Meditation

Day 14: Understanding Your Emotional Triggers

- **Today's Reflection Prompt:**

"What specific situations, places, or people trigger this emotion strongly for me?"

....

....

- **Today's Affirmation:**

"Understanding my triggers gives me power over my emotional responses."

- **Mini-Challenge:**

Write down clearly one emotional trigger you experienced today and how you responded.

....

- **Daily Check-in:**
  How aware was I today when this emotion surfaced?
  [1 (Not aware) — 5 (Very aware)] _____

Day 15: The Hidden Message in Your Emotions

- **Today's Reflection Prompt:**
  "What might this emotional trap be trying to teach me or protect me from?"

....

....

- **Today's Affirmation:**
  "I listen to my emotions with openness and curiosity."

- **Mini-Challenge:**
  Reflect briefly on a situation today when you felt this emotion. Ask yourself: "What is this feeling really about?"

....

- **Meditation Moment:**
  (Visualize gently accepting and understanding your emotion, without judgment.)

Day 16: Reframing Your Emotional Story

- **Today's Reflection Prompt:**
  "Reflecting on Jay Jordan's story, how could viewing my emotions differently empower me rather than trap me?"

....

....

- **Today's Affirmation:**
  "I reframe my emotional story to empower myself."

- **Mini-Challenge:**
  Write down one empowering way to view your emotion. For example:
  "My fear reminds me I'm courageous; my shame shows me my capacity for growth."

- **Daily Tracker:**
  | Emotion Reframed ☐ | Affirmation Recited ☐ | Journal Completed ☐ |

Day 17: Breaking the Emotional Cycle

- **Today's Reflection Prompt:**
  "What small, positive action can I take next time this emotion appears, to break its hold on me?"

....

....

- **Today's Affirmation:**
  "I take proactive steps to break free from emotional traps."

- **Action Step:**
  Identify one specific action or response you will try next time you feel trapped emotionally:

- **My Action Step:** _____

- **Meditation Moment (2 min):**
  (Visualize yourself successfully breaking free from the emotional trap.)

Day 18: Weekly Reflection & Milestone Celebration

- **Today's Reflection Prompt:**
  "What meaningful insights or changes have I experienced by clearly facing and understanding my emotional traps this week?"

....

....

- **Today's Affirmation:**
  "Facing my emotions has made me stronger and clearer."

- **Milestone Celebration:**

Write one significant emotional insight or achievement you're proud of this week:

My Milestone: _____

- **Community Connection (Optional but Encouraged):**

Share this week's emotional insight or milestone with someone supportive. Who can I share with? _____

Week 3 Summary:

- **Primary emotional trap identified:**

....

....

....

....

- **New understanding of my emotional triggers:**

....

....

....

....

- **Most helpful emotional reframing this week:**

....

....

....

....

Preparing for Next Week:

Next, we'll work on shifting your mindset from "victim" to "leader." You'll learn to reclaim your power by taking full responsibility for your future.

You're moving beyond emotional traps. Each step brings you closer to freedom.

Week 4: Shifting from Victim to Leader Mindset (Section 1.4)

Weekly Focus:

This week, you'll work on shifting your mindset from feeling powerless (victim) to recognizing your ability to take control and lead your own life. Taking full responsibility for your choices—without shame—empowers you to step into leadership over your own future.

Remember:

Jay Jordan had every reason to believe he was stuck in a system designed to hold him back. But instead of allowing his past to define him, he took ownership of his mindset and decisions. Your transformation begins when you recognize your power.

Day 19: Recognizing Where You've Felt Powerless

- **Today's Reflection Prompt:**
  "Where in my life have I felt powerless or stuck? What areas do I believe are out of my control?"

....

....

- **Today's Affirmation:**
  "I acknowledge where I've felt powerless, but I am ready to change."

- **Mini-Challenge:**
  Notice one moment today where you feel powerless. Instead of reacting automatically, pause and reflect on whether there's a small action you can take to reclaim some control.

- **Daily Tracker:**
  | Affirmation Recited ☐ | Powerless Moment Recognized ☐ | Journal Completed ☐ |

- **Meditation Moment (2–3 min):**
  Breathe deeply and affirm: "I have more power than I realize."
  ☐ Completed Meditation

Day 20: The Truth About Responsibility vs. Blame

- **Today's Reflection Prompt:**
  "What's the difference between taking responsibility for my future and blaming myself for my past?"

....

....

- **Today's Affirmation:**
  "Taking responsibility empowers me; it does not blame me."

- **Mini-Challenge:**
  Write down one way you can take responsibility for your future today without guilt or self-blame.

....

- **Daily Check-in:**
  How did it feel to take ownership today?

  [1 (Difficult) — 5 (Empowering)] _____

Day 21: Reframing Your Identity as a Leader

- **Today's Reflection Prompt:**
  "How would I describe myself if my past mistakes and circumstances didn't define me? What kind of leader do I want to become in my own life?"

....

....

- **Today's Affirmation:**
  "I am rewriting my story as a leader of my own life."

- **Mini-Challenge:**
  Write a Leader Identity Statement, beginning with "I am…"

- **Example:**
- "I am a person who makes strong, intentional choices and creates opportunities for myself and others."

- **Meditation Moment:**

(Visualize yourself standing strong as a leader, making decisions with confidence.)

Day 22: Overcoming the Fear of Leadership

- **Today's Reflection Prompt:**

"What fears come up when I think about taking full responsibility for my life and stepping into leadership?"

....

....

- **Today's Affirmation:**

"I release my fear of leading my own life."

- **Mini-Challenge:**

Challenge your fear by taking one action today that reinforces leadership.

  - **Example Actions:**
  - Speak up about what you need.
  - Make a clear decision without overthinking.
  - Set a boundary with confidence.
- **Daily Tracker:**

  | Fear Identified ☐ | Leadership Action Taken ☐ | Journal Completed ☐ |

Day 23: Choosing Ownership Over Excuses

- **Today's Reflection Prompt:**

"What excuses do I tend to use when I avoid taking control of my life? How can I reframe those excuses into responsibility?"

....

- **Today's Affirmation:**

"I replace excuses with responsibility."

- **Mini-Challenge:**

Identify one excuse you've been using recently and reframe it into an empowering statement.

  - **Example:** "I can't succeed because no one gives me a chance."
  - **Reframe:** "I will create my own opportunities."
  - **Excuse:** _____
  - **Reframe:** _____

- **Meditation Moment:**

(Picture yourself boldly moving past the excuses of your past.)

Day 24: Weekly Reflection & Milestone Celebration

- **Today's Reflection Prompt:**

"What is one way I've stepped into leadership over my life this week?"

- **Today's Affirmation:**

"Every day, I am becoming a stronger leader of my own future."

- **Milestone Celebration:**

Write down a leadership moment you had this week:

  - **My Leadership Moment:** _____

  Community Connection (Optional but Encouraged):

Who in my life models leadership in a way I admire? How can I learn from them?

Week 4 Summary:

- **One way I took responsibility this week:**

....

....

....

....

- **An excuse I transformed into an empowering mindset:**

....

....

....

....

- **A moment I saw myself as a leader:**

....

....

....

....

Preparing for Next Week:

Next, you'll focus on the final transformation—resetting your mindset and making success your new normal. By reinforcing your new identity, you'll make these changes **automatic and sustainable.**

Stepping into leadership isn't about perfection—it's about choosing, every day, to take responsibility for your future.

Week 5: Resetting Your Mindset for Transformation (Section 1.5 – Action Plan)

Weekly Focus:

This is your moment of **commitment**. After uncovering hidden scripts, breaking free from self-sabotage, and shifting from victim to leader, this week you will **solidify your transformation** with concrete actions and create a **sustainable plan** for lasting success.

Remember:

True transformation isn't just about knowing what needs to change—it's about doing the work consistently. Your future self is built by the actions you take today.

Day 25: Defining Your New Identity

- **Today's Reflection Prompt:**
  "Who am I becoming now that I've broken free from my old patterns? What are the qualities of my future self?"

....

....

- **Today's Affirmation:**
  "I am stepping fully into my new, empowered identity."

- **Mini-Challenge:**
  Write a statement of identity that clearly defines your new mindset.
  Example: "I am a person who takes control of my future, makes intentional choices, and never lets my past define me."

....

- **Daily Tracker:**
  | Identity Statement Written ☐ | Affirmation Recited ☐ | Journal Completed ☐ |

- **Meditation Moment (2–3 min):**
  Breathe deeply and visualize your new self stepping confidently into your future.
  ☐ Completed Meditation

Day 26: Creating a Mindset Reset Ritual

- **Today's Reflection Prompt:**
  "What specific habits or routines can I build into my daily life to reinforce my new mindset?"

....

- **Today's Affirmation:**
  "I set myself up for success with consistent habits."

- **Mini-Challenge:**
  Design a daily mindset reset ritual (2–5 minutes long) that you can commit to.

  - **Example Ritual:**
  - Morning affirmation
  - Quick meditation or deep breathing
  - Reviewing your daily goal or habit tracker

- **Daily Check-in:**
  Which part of my new ritual felt most empowering today?

Day 27: Identifying and Preventing Relapse Triggers

- **Today's Reflection Prompt:**
  "What situations or emotions could tempt me to fall back into my old patterns?"

- **Today's Affirmation:**
  "I anticipate challenges and respond with strength."

- **Mini-Challenge:**
  List three potential relapse triggers and create an action plan for overcoming them.

  - **Example:**
  - **Trigger:** Feeling overwhelmed → **Response:** Take a 5-minute break, breathe, and refocus.
  - Trigger:_____ →Response: _____
  - Trigger:_____ →Response: _____
  - Trigger:_____ →Response: _____

- **Meditation Moment:**
  Visualize yourself confidently handling one of these triggers with ease.

Day 28: Setting Short-Term & Long-Term Goals

- **Today's Reflection Prompt:**
  "What short-term goal (30-60 days) and long-term goal (1 year) will help me sustain this transformation?"

....

....

- **Today's Affirmation:**
  "I set clear goals and take action toward them every day."

- **Mini-Challenge:**
  Write down one short-term goal and one long-term goal, ensuring they are specific and achievable. Example:

  - **Short-Term Goal (30 days):** Stick to my morning mindset ritual every day.
  - **Long-Term Goal (1 year):** Build financial stability by securing steady employment.
  - **Short-Term Goal (30 days):** _____
  - **Long-Term Goal (1 year):** _____

- **Daily Tracker:**
  | Goals Written ☐ | Affirmation Recited ☐ | Journal Completed ☐ |

- **Meditation Moment:**
  Picture yourself one year from now, having achieved your goals.

Day 29: Accountability & Support Systems

- **Today's Reflection Prompt:**
  "Who can I lean on for encouragement, guidance, or accountability as I continue my journey?"

....

- **Today's Affirmation:**

  "I welcome support and accountability into my life."

- **Mini-Challenge:**

  Identify one person or community who can support you. Reach out to them today and share your commitment.

- **Daily Check-in:**

  How did it feel to involve someone in my transformation?

Day 30: Celebration & Commitment Letter to My Future Self

- **Today's Reflection Prompt:**

  "What are the biggest mindset shifts I've experienced over the last 30 days? How do I feel different?"

- **Today's Affirmation:**

  "I am committed to my transformation for the long term."

- **Final Mini-Challenge:**

  Write a letter to your future self, describing what you've learned, how you feel, and your commitment to staying on this path. (Space at back of this workbook.)

- **Milestone Celebration:**

  Write down one major personal breakthrough that happened in the last 30 days.

- **Community Connection (Optional but Encouraged):**

  Consider sharing part of your journey with someone who has supported you.

Week 5 Summary: (Final Check-In)

- **The biggest mindset shift I've experienced is:**

....

....

....

....

- **My new identity statement is:**

....

....

....

....

- **The daily ritual I commit to is:**

....

....

....

....

- **The biggest lesson I will carry forward is:**

....

....

....

....

Moving Forward: Your Next Steps

You've just completed a powerful 30-day journey of self-discovery and transformation. Over the past five weeks, you've uncovered **hidden subconscious scripts, broken free from self-sabotage, confronted emotional traps, and shifted from a victim mindset to a leader mentality.** Most importantly, you've taken action—not just by thinking about change, but by **actively choosing it every day.**

Now, you're ready for the next step.

Recognizing old patterns is the first breakthrough, but real transformation happens when you **rewire your brain to make these new beliefs automatic.** In **Chapter 2,** you'll learn **the science behind lasting change—how habits form, how to reprogram your brain for success, and how small daily actions create unshakable momentum.**

This next 30-day challenge will take your breakthroughs from Chapter 1 and reinforce them through neuroscience-backed strategies, so that the progress you've made doesn't fade—**it becomes your new reality.**

Let's get started—your brain is ready for its upgrade.

Chapter 2

Rewiring Your Brain for Success

"If I could change, you can too." — Shaka Senghor

In Chapter 1, you uncovered the thought patterns and habits that held you back. You recognized the emotional traps and self-sabotaging behaviors that kept you stuck. You even began shifting from a victim mentality to a leader mindset—choosing to take responsibility for your future.

Now, it's time for the next step: **rewiring your brain for success.**

This isn't just about thinking positively—it's about using science-backed strategies to actually retrain your mind and body to support your growth.

Shaka Senghor, who spent 19 years in prison, once believed he was doomed to repeat the cycles of violence and failure that had shaped his life. But while incarcerated, he discovered the power of **neuroplasticity**—the brain's ability to change and grow when given the right input.

He studied daily, visualized his future self, and practiced gratitude—until his brain believed in his success before it even happened. This mental transformation was the first step in breaking free—not just from prison, but from the mental barriers that had controlled his life.

Your mind is your most powerful weapon.

You don't need luck. You don't need a perfect past. You just need the right mindset and habits.

In the next 30 days, you'll:

- Understand how your brain actually works (neuroscience, not guesswork)

- Rewire negative thought patterns by replacing them with success-driven ones

- Use visualization, affirmations, and daily action to create automatic momentum

- Apply simple but powerful daily exercises to make progress feel natural

If Shaka Senghor could rebuild his mind under the most challenging circumstances, **so can you.**

Let's start rewiring your brain for success.

Week 1: Understanding Neuroplasticity & Training Your Brain for Success (Section 2.1)

Weekly Focus:

Your brain is not fixed. It adapts, changes, and rewires based on the thoughts you feed it and the habits you practice. This week, you'll learn how to train your mind like an athlete trains his body—so that success becomes second nature.

Remember:

If your past thoughts and habits created a cycle of struggle, your new thoughts and habits can create a cycle of success.

Day 1: Your Brain Can Change (Neuroplasticity 101)

- **Today's Reflection Prompt:**
  "What negative thought patterns or behaviors have shaped my life? How did I learn these patterns?"

....

....

- **Today's Affirmation:**
  "I have the power to rewire my brain and reshape my future."

- **Mini-Challenge:**
  Write down one habit or belief that has held you back.

  - **Example:** "I believe I will always struggle."

....

  - Success begins with what you tell yourself every day.

- **Daily Tracker:**
  | Affirmation Recited ☐ | Thought Pattern Identified ☐ | Journal Completed ☐ |

- **Meditation Moment (2–3 min):**
  Breathe deeply and affirm: "Every thought I choose strengthens my new mindset."
  ☐ Completed Meditation

Day 2: Breaking the Cycle of Negative Thought Loops

- **Today's Reflection Prompt:**

  "What thoughts do I repeat daily that keep me stuck? Where did these beliefs start?"

  ....

  ....

- **Today's Affirmation:**

  "I am aware of my thoughts, and I choose which ones to keep."

- **Mini-Challenge:**

  Write down one common negative thought and its positive replacement.

  - **Example:**
  - **Negative Thought:** "I will always fail."
  - **Replacement Thought:** "Every setback is a lesson that brings me closer to success."
  - **Negative Thought:** _____
  - **Replacement Thought:** _____

- What you think every day becomes what you believe, and what you believe becomes reality.

Day 3: The Power of Mental Rehearsal

- **Today's Reflection Prompt:**

  "If I were already successful, how would I think, feel, and act?"

  ....

  ....

- **Today's Affirmation:**

  "I see myself as successful, and my brain aligns with that vision."

- **Mini-Challenge:**

  Visualize yourself achieving a major goal. Write down three details about what you see, feel, or hear in that vision.

  Your mind creates your reality.

Day 4: Training Your Brain for Motivation (Dopamine & Reward Systems)

- **Today's Reflection Prompt:**
  "What activities make me feel accomplished or motivated? How can I use that to fuel my growth?"

....

....

- **Today's Affirmation:**
  "I train my brain to crave progress and success."

- **Mini-Challenge:**
  Choose one action today that gives you a small dopamine boost

  Example: Completing a workout, reading 5 pages, making a positive decision.

Day 5: Creating Automatic Success Patterns

- **Today's Reflection Prompt:**
  "What daily habits can I create to reinforce my new mindset?"

....

....

- **Today's Affirmation:**
  "Every action I take rewires my brain for success."

- **Mini-Challenge:**
  Write out one simple morning habit that will reinforce your new mindset.
  Example: "Each morning, I will repeat my affirmations."

....

Day 6: Weekly Reflection & Milestone Celebration

- **Today's Reflection Prompt:**
  "What is one new thought, habit, or behavior I've actively changed this week?"

....

- **Today's Affirmation:**
  "I acknowledge and celebrate my progress, no matter how small."

- **Milestone Celebration:**
  Write down one major realization or mindset shift from this week:
  Example: "I realize I can catch my negative thoughts before they spiral."

....

- **Community Connection (Optional but Encouraged):**
  Who can I share this progress with? _____

Week 1 Summary:

- **Biggest mindset shift this week:**

....

....

....

....

- **New habit I will continue reinforcing:**

....

....

....

....

- **One thing I've learned about my brain's ability to change:**

....

....

....

....

Final Thought Before Week 2:

Shaka Senghor changed his life by changing his mind—before he even left prison.

If he could train his brain for success under those circumstances, what's stopping you from doing the same?

Next week, we'll take what you've learned and turn it into consistent, success-building habits.

Your mind is already changing. Keep feeding it the right thoughts.

Week 2: Breaking the Habit of Being Your Old Self (Section 2.2)

Weekly Focus:

Last week, you learned how **neuroplasticity** allows you to rewire your brain. But here's the challenge: Your old self—the version of you shaped by past experiences, bad habits, and limiting beliefs—will try to pull you back.

This week, your goal is to **break free from the patterns of your old self** and start **living as the person you are becoming.**

Remember:

Your brain defaults to what is familiar. If you want change, you must make success feel like home.

Shaka Senghor didn't just **think differently**—he **acted differently. He studied, spoke, and moved as the leader he wanted to be**—even when no one saw it yet.

This week, you'll do the same.

Day 7: Recognizing the Pull of the Old Self

- **Today's Reflection Prompt:**
  "When do I feel most tempted to return to my old habits and mindset? What situations trigger these urges?"

....

....

- **Today's Affirmation:**

"I am aware of my old patterns, but I am not controlled by them."

- **Mini-Challenge:**

Identify one moment today when you feel yourself slipping into an old habit or mindset. Pause and write about it.

....

....

- **Daily Tracker:**

| Old Pattern Noticed ☐ | Affirmation Recited ☐ | Journal Completed ☐ |

- **Meditation Moment (2–3 min):**

Breathe deeply and remind yourself: "I am not my past—I am my choices today."
☐ Completed Meditation

Day 8: Disrupting Automatic Negative Behaviors

- **Today's Reflection Prompt:**

"What daily behaviors reinforce my old self? What small action can I take today to disrupt them?"

....

....

- **Today's Affirmation:**

"I am conscious of my choices and I make new, empowered decisions."

- **Mini-Challenge:**

Choose one behavior to disrupt today.
Example:

- If you wake up and immediately scroll social media, replace it with 5 minutes of affirmations or goal review.

Every small decision to disrupt the old self adds up.

Day 9: Interrupting Negative Thought Loops

- **Today's Reflection Prompt:**
  "What recurring negative thought tries to keep me stuck? How can I interrupt it today?"

....

....

- **Today's Affirmation:**
  "I reject thoughts that do not serve my growth."

- **Mini-Challenge:**
  The next time your old thought appears, interrupt it immediately.

  - Say "Stop" in your mind.

  - Replace it with an intentional new thought.

- **Example:**
  - **Negative Thought:** "I always mess things up."

  - **Interruption:** Say "STOP."

  - **New Thought:** "I am constantly improving."

- **Daily Tracker:**
  | Thought Interruption Completed ☐ | Affirmation Recited ☐ | Journal Completed ☐ |

- **Meditation Moment:**
  (Visualize yourself shutting down a negative thought and replacing it with a new one.)

Day 10: Embodying the New You – Moving & Thinking Differently

- **Today's Reflection Prompt:**
  "If I were already successful, how would I think, speak, and act differently?"

....

....

- **Today's Affirmation:**
  "I step into my new self with confidence."

- **Mini-Challenge:**

Physically act as your future self today.

- Walk taller.

- Speak clearly.

- Make one decision based on your future self, not your old self.

- **Daily Tracker:**
  | Action Taken as Future Self ☐ | Affirmation Recited ☐ | Journal Completed ☐ |

- **Meditation Moment:**
  Visualize yourself fully embodying your new identity.)

Day 11: Eliminating Triggers That Reinforce the Old You

- **Today's Reflection Prompt:**
  "What environments, people, or habits reinforce my old identity? How can I reduce their influence?"

....

....

- **Today's Affirmation:**
  "I create a space that supports my transformation."

- **Mini-Challenge:**
  Identify one external trigger that reinforces your old habits.
  Example:

  - If negative people bring you down, limit contact today.

  - If certain places reinforce old habits, change your routine.

- **Meditation Moment:**
  (Visualize clearing space for the new you to grow.)

Day 12: Weekly Reflection & Milestone Celebration

- **Today's Reflection Prompt:**
  "What is one old habit or behavior I successfully interrupted this week?"

....

....

- **Today's Affirmation:**

  "I am committed to becoming the best version of myself."

- **Milestone Celebration:**

  Write down one major shift in your thinking or behavior from this week.

  Example: "I noticed negative thoughts and replaced them immediately."

....

- **Community Connection (Optional but Encouraged):**

  Who in my life can I share my progress with? _____

Week 2 Summary:

- **One habit or thought pattern I successfully disrupted:**

....

....

....

....

- **One way I acted as my future self this week:**

....

....

....

- **One trigger I am committed to eliminating:**

....

....

....

....

Preparing for Next Week:

You are actively breaking the habit of being your old self.

The next step? **Replacing those old patterns with powerful success habits.**

Your past does not define you. Your choices today create your future.

Week 3: The Success Mindset Formula (Section 2.3)

Weekly Focus:

Success isn't random—it follows **a formula.** Highly successful people **think, act, and make decisions in a way that consistently moves them forward.**

This week, you'll learn the **Success Mindset Formula,** so you can **apply it to your own life** and build an unstoppable mentality.

Remember:

Success is not about luck—it's about mindset, strategy, and consistency.

Shaka Senghor built his success by following **a mental formula that kept him focused, disciplined, and resilient.** This week, you'll do the same.

Day 13: Defining the Success Mindset

- **Today's Reflection Prompt:**
  "What does success mean to me personally? How would my life look if I had already achieved it?"

....

....

- **Today's Affirmation:**
  "Success begins in my mind before it happens in my life."

- **Mini-Challenge:**

Write your own definition of success in one sentence.

Example: "Success means having control over my choices and creating a future I'm proud of."

....

....

- **Daily Tracker:**
  | Success Definition Written ☐ | Affirmation Recited ☐ | Journal Completed ☐ |

- **Meditation Moment (2–3 min):**
  Breathe deeply and affirm: "I am designing my success, step by step."
  ☐ Completed Meditation

Day 14: The 4 Key Components of a Success Mindset

- **Today's Reflection Prompt:**
  "Which of these four components do I struggle with most: belief, discipline, adaptability, or persistence?"

....

....

- **Today's Affirmation:**
  "I am developing the mindset of a successful person."

- **Mini-Challenge:**
  Identify one area to improve in your success mindset formula.
  Example: "I need to improve my adaptability when facing setbacks."

- **Daily Tracker:**
  | Success Component Identified ☐ | Affirmation Recited ☐ | Journal Completed ☐ |

- **Meditation Moment:**
  (Visualize yourself embodying the four success components.)

Day 15: Building Unshakable Self-Belief

- **Today's Reflection Prompt:**
  "What self-doubt has held me back in the past? How can I reframe it into self-belief?"

  ....

  ....

- **Today's Affirmation:**
  "I trust in my ability to succeed, even when challenges arise."

- **Mini-Challenge:**
  Write down one past challenge you overcame, proving your ability to succeed.

  ....

  ....

Day 16: Developing Unbreakable Discipline

- **Today's Reflection Prompt:**
  "Where in my life do I lack consistency? How can I create more discipline?"

  ....

  ....

- **Today's Affirmation:**
  "Discipline is my superpower—I do what needs to be done, no matter what."

- **Mini-Challenge:**
  Identify one area where you will commit to discipline today.
  Example: "I will wake up 30 minutes earlier to work on my goals."

- **Meditation Moment:**
  (Picture yourself executing your goals with strong discipline.)

Day 17: Embracing Adaptability & Persistence

- **Today's Reflection Prompt:**

"How do I usually react to setbacks? What can I do differently next time I face a challenge?"

....

....

- **Today's Affirmation:**
  "I see obstacles as opportunities to grow."

- **Mini-Challenge:**
  Think about a past failure. How can you reframe it as a lesson?
  Example: "My past job loss wasn't failure—it was a chance to realign with my true path."

Day 18: Weekly Reflection & Milestone Celebration

- **Today's Reflection Prompt:**
  "What part of the Success Mindset Formula has had the biggest impact on me this week?"

- **Today's Affirmation:**
  "I am building the mindset of a leader and a winner."

- **Milestone Celebration:**
  Write one shift in your mindset from this week.
  Example: "I no longer see challenges as stopping points—I see them as growth points."

- **Community Connection (Optional but Encouraged):**
  Who can I share my mindset shift with? _____

Week 3 Summary:

- **One major mindset shift I experienced:**

....

....

....

....

- **One area of success mindset I improved:**

....

....

....

- **One way I'm practicing discipline daily:**

....

....

....

Preparing for Next Week:

You are developing the mindset of a successful person.

Next, we'll focus on **training your brain for focus, discipline, and momentum**.

Your success formula is already working—keep applying it.

Week 4: Hacking Your Brain Chemistry for Motivation and Focus (Section 2.4)

Weekly Focus:

By now, you've learned how to **retrain your brain for success, break old habits, and develop a winning mindset.** But even the strongest mindset can struggle without **consistent motivation and focus.**

The good news? Your brain is wired to help you—**if you know how to use it.**

This week, you'll learn how to **hack your brain's chemistry** so that motivation and focus become **natural, automatic, and sustainable.**

Remember:

Motivation isn't about willpower—it's about understanding your brain and using it to your advantage.

Shaka Senghor didn't rely on **motivation alone** to change his life. He trained his mind to **stay focused, create structure, and use dopamine rewards to reinforce his new identity.**

This week, you'll do the same.

Day 19: Understanding Dopamine – The Key to Motivation

- **Today's Reflection Prompt:**
  "What activities make me feel motivated and energized? How can I use them to create momentum?"

....

....

- **Today's Affirmation:**
  "I train my brain to crave progress and success."

- **Mini-Challenge:**
  Identify one dopamine-boosting habit to reinforce progress.
  Example: Completing a small task and celebrating with a fist pump or deep breath of accomplishment.

- **Daily Tracker:**
  | Dopamine Habit Identified ☐ | Affirmation Recited ☐ | Journal Completed ☐ |

- **Meditation Moment (2–3 min):**
  Breathe deeply and remind yourself: "I create my own motivation by taking action."
  ☐ Completed Meditation

Day 20: The Action-First Rule – Motivation Follows Movement

- **Today's Reflection Prompt:**
  "When do I wait for motivation before taking action? How can I reverse that pattern?"

....

- **Today's Affirmation:**

"Action creates motivation—I move first, then my brain follows."

- **Mini-Challenge:**

Take one small action before you feel "ready."

Example: Start your workout, open your book, or make a to-do list—even if you don't feel like it.

Day 21: Managing Distractions – Training Your Focus Muscle

- **Today's Reflection Prompt:**

"What are my biggest distractions? How can I eliminate or reduce them?"

- **Today's Affirmation:**

"I train my brain to stay focused and disciplined."

- **Mini-Challenge:**

Identify one major distraction and create a plan to remove or reduce it.

Example:

- Phone distractions? Use "Do Not Disturb" mode for 1 hour.

- **Meditation Moment:**

(Visualize yourself fully focused, free from distractions.)

Day 22: Using the 90-Minute Focus Rule

- **Today's Reflection Prompt:**

"When do I feel most focused during the day? How can I structure my time for deep work?"

- **Today's Affirmation:**

"I optimize my focus by working in deep, intentional time blocks."

- **Mini-Challenge:**
  Try one 90-minute deep work session today.

  - Set a timer, remove distractions, and work on a meaningful task.

- **Daily Tracker:**
  | 90-Minute Focus Session Completed ☐ | Affirmation Recited ☐ | Journal Completed ☐ |

Day 23: Leveraging Rewards and Celebration for Long-Term Motivation

- **Today's Reflection Prompt:**
  "What small rewards can I use to reinforce positive habits and discipline?"

....

....

- **Today's Affirmation:**
  "I train my brain to associate success with positive reinforcement."

- **Mini-Challenge:**
  Choose a reward system to reinforce focus and discipline.
  Example:

  After completing a big task, treat yourself to 5 minutes of music, a walk, or something enjoyable.

Day 24: Weekly Reflection & Milestone Celebration

- **Today's Reflection Prompt:**
  "What brain hacks helped me stay motivated and focused this week?"

....

....

- **Today's Affirmation:**
  "I am mastering my brain and using it to fuel my success."

- **Milestone Celebration:**
  Write down one mental breakthrough from this week.
  Example: "I realized motivation follows action, not the other way around."

- **Community Connection (Optional but Encouraged):**
  Who can I share this insight with? _____

Week 4 Summary:

- **One brain hack that improved my focus:**

....

....

....

....

- **One distraction I eliminated or reduced:**

....

....

....

....

- **One reward system I will continue using:**

....

....

....

....

Preparing for Next Week:

You are now in control of your brain's motivation and focus.

Next, we'll focus on **turning your new mindset and habits into a lifelong identity.**

Your brain works for you—train it to help you win.

Week 5: The Action Plan for Rewiring Your Brain (Section 2.5)

Weekly Focus:

This week, you will put everything from **Chapter 2** into action with a structured plan. The goal? To **solidify your transformation and make success automatic.**

You now understand:

- How **neuroplasticity** allows you to rewire your mind

- How to **break the habit of being your old self**

- The **Success Mindset Formula** and how to apply it

- How to **hack your brain chemistry for motivation and focus**

Now, we'll take those lessons and turn them into a long-term action plan.

Remember:

Success doesn't happen overnight—but small, consistent actions lead to massive transformation.

Day 25: Defining Your New Identity

- **Today's Reflection Prompt:**

   "Who am I now that I've rewired my brain for success? What qualities define my new identity?"

....

....

- **Today's Affirmation:**

   "I fully embrace my new identity as a strong, disciplined, and focused person."

- **Mini-Challenge:**

   Write an identity statement that reflects your transformation.

   Example: "I am a person who thinks with clarity, acts with purpose, and stays committed to my growth."

....

....

- **Daily Tracker:**

  | Identity Statement Written ☐ | Affirmation Recited ☐ | Journal Completed ☐ |

- **Meditation Moment (2–3 min):**

  Breathe deeply and visualize yourself fully stepping into your new identity.

  ☐ Completed Meditation

Day 26: Creating Your Daily Success Routine

- **Today's Reflection Prompt:**

  "What habits do I need in my daily routine to reinforce my success mindset?"

  ....

  ....

- **Today's Affirmation:**

  "My daily habits are shaping my future."

- **Mini-Challenge:**

  Design a simple morning and evening routine that supports your transformation.

  Example:

  - **Morning Routine:** Affirmations, goal review, 10 minutes of learning.
  - **Evening Routine:** Reflection, gratitude, planning tomorrow's priorities.
  - **Morning Routine:** _____
  - **Evening Routine:** _____

- **Meditation Moment:**

  (Visualize yourself executing your new routine effortlessly.)

Day 27: Identifying and Preventing Setbacks

- **Today's Reflection Prompt:**

  "What obstacles or situations might make me fall back into old patterns? How will I handle them?"

  ....

  ....

- **Today's Affirmation:**

  "I am prepared for challenges, and I overcome them with confidence."

- **Mini-Challenge:**

  Write a setback prevention plan with specific actions for when obstacles arise.

  Example:

  - If I feel unmotivated → I will take one small action anyway.

  - If I get distracted → I will remove the distraction and refocus.

  - If I_____ → I will_____

  - If I_____ → I will_____

Day 28: Setting Short-Term and Long-Term Goals

- **Today's Reflection Prompt:**

  "What are my most important short-term (30-90 days) and long-term (1-5 years) goals?"

  ....

  ....

- **Today's Affirmation:**

  "I set clear goals and take action toward them every day."

- **Mini-Challenge:**

  Write one short-term goal and one long-term goal with a clear first step to achieving them.

  Example:

  - **Short-term goal:** Secure a job in 60 days → Step 1: Update my resume today.

  - **Long-term goal:** Build financial security → Step 1: Start saving $20 per paycheck.

  - **Short-term goal:**_____

  - **Long-term goal:**_____

- **Daily Tracker:**

  | Goals Written ☐ | Affirmation Recited ☐ | Journal Completed ☐ |

- **Meditation Moment:**

  (Picture yourself achieving your short- and long-term goals.)

Day 29: Accountability & Support Systems

- **Today's Reflection Prompt:**

  "Who can I rely on for accountability and support in my journey?"

  ....

  ....

- **Today's Affirmation:**

  "I surround myself with people who encourage and challenge me."

- **Mini-Challenge:**

  Identify one accountability partner or support system and commit to checking in with them.

Day 30: Celebration & Commitment to Your Future Self

- **Today's Reflection Prompt:**

  "What are the biggest mindset shifts I've experienced in the last 30 days?"

- **Today's Affirmation:**

  "I am committed to my success for life."

- **Final Mini-Challenge:**

  Write a letter to your future self, describing what you've learned, how you feel, and your commitment to your new path. (Space at back of this workbook.)

- **Milestone Celebration:**

  Write down one major breakthrough you've had in the last 30 days.

  ....

  ....

- **Community Connection (Optional but Encouraged):**

  Who can I share my growth with? _____

Week 5 Summary: (Final Check-In)

- **The biggest mindset shift I've experienced is:**

....

....

....

....

- **My new identity statement is:**

....

....

....

....

- **The daily routine I commit to is:**

....

....

....

....

- **The biggest lesson I will carry forward is:**

....

....

....

....

You've just completed an intense 30-day journey in rewiring your brain for success. Through the power of **neuroplasticity**, you've proven that you are capable of **breaking old patterns, adopting a success mindset, and training your brain for focus, motivation, and resilience.**

Over the past five weeks, you have:

- **Reprogrammed your thoughts** to align with your goals.
- **Learned to break the habit of being your old self** and step into your new identity.
- **Mastered the Success Mindset Formula** to keep yourself moving forward.
- **Hacked your brain's chemistry** to create motivation and focus on demand.
- **Developed a concrete action plan** to sustain your transformation.

But transformation doesn't stop with the mind—it's time to **face the fears that have held you back for far too long.**

In **Chapter 3**, you'll confront **fear, self-doubt, and insecurity** head-on. You'll learn how to **rewrite your fear response, shift your self-perception, and build unshakable confidence.**

Now it's time to strip fear of its power and take your transformation to the next level.

Let's begin—your next breakthrough is **on the other side of fear.**

Chapter 3

Overcoming Fear and Self-Doubt—Breaking the Chains Holding You Back

Fear is not meant to stop you. It's meant to be understood.

Fear is one of the most powerful forces in life—it has the ability to **protect us, but also to paralyze us.** If you're reading this, you've likely experienced the kind of fear that **keeps you stuck,** afraid to take the next step, afraid to believe in your own potential.

But here's the truth: **Fear is learned, which means it can also be unlearned.**

Few people understand the weight of fear and self-doubt more than **Monica Lewinsky.** At just 22 years old, she found herself at the center of one of the biggest scandals in modern history. Her name became a **punchline, a cautionary tale, and a symbol of public shaming.**

For years, **fear and humiliation kept her silent.** She lived in the shadow of her past, afraid that no matter what she did, she would always be defined by her mistakes. **The world had made up its mind about her— could she change the narrative?**

The answer was **yes.**

She took control of her story by stepping into **advocacy, speaking out against cyberbullying and public shaming.** Instead of being destroyed by her past, she used it as **fuel for a new purpose.** She redefined herself—not as a victim of public scrutiny, but as a leader in the conversation about how we treat people who make mistakes.

This chapter is about **breaking free from fear and self-doubt so you can move forward with confidence, clarity, and courage.**

In the next 30 days, you'll:

- Identify and understand the root causes of your fears.
- Rewire your brain's fear response so fear no longer controls you.
- Replace self-doubt with confidence-building habits.
- Develop the courage to take action despite fear.

You've already proven you're capable of change. Now, it's time to **conquer the mental barriers standing between you and the future you deserve.**

Let's start by understanding where fear truly comes from.

Week 1: Understanding the Root of Fear (Section 3.1)

Weekly Focus:

Fear doesn't just appear out of nowhere. It's **learned, reinforced, and stored deep in your subconscious mind.** This week, you'll uncover the **real reasons behind your fears** and learn how to **separate real fear from imagined limitations.**

Remember:
Fear isn't the enemy. Staying stuck because of fear is.

Monica Lewinsky spent years **afraid to be seen, to speak out, to take control of her life.** But the moment she **understood her fear rather than running from it, she took back her power.**

This week, you will do the same.

Day 1: Identifying Your Core Fears

- **Today's Reflection Prompt:**
  "What specific fear has held me back the most in my life? How has it shaped my decisions?"

....

....

- **Today's Affirmation:**
  "I am brave enough to face my fears head-on."

- **Mini-Challenge:**
  Write down your #1 fear and how it has impacted your life.

....

- **Daily Tracker:**
  | Fear Identified ☐ | Affirmation Recited ☐ | Journal Completed ☐ |

- **Meditation Moment (2–3 min):**

Breathe deeply and remind yourself: "Fear is a teacher, not a master."
☐ Completed Meditation

Day 2: Where Does Fear Come From?

- **Today's Reflection Prompt:**

  "When did this fear first begin? Was it taught to me by someone else or shaped by my experiences?"

  ....

  ....

- **Today's Affirmation:**

  "I release the fears that no longer serve me."

- **Mini-Challenge:**

  Identify the origin of your fear and write down one way you can start letting go of it.

  ....

- **Meditation Moment:**

  (Visualize yourself removing fear like an old coat you no longer need.)

Day 3: Distinguishing Real Fear from Mental Blocks

- **Today's Reflection Prompt:**

  "Is my fear protecting me from real danger, or is it keeping me from growth?"

  ....

  ....

- **Today's Affirmation:**

  "I trust myself to know the difference between real fear and self-imposed limits."

- **Mini-Challenge:**

  Write down one fear you realize is NOT a real danger, but just a mental block.
  Example: Fear of failure → The truth is, failure is part of success.

  ....

- **Daily Tracker:**

| Fear Analyzed ☐ | Affirmation Recited ☐ | Journal Completed ☐ |

Day 4: Rewriting Your Fear Story

- **Today's Reflection Prompt:**

"If I weren't afraid, how would my life be different? What would I do differently today?"

....

....

- **Today's Affirmation:**

"I choose courage over fear in every decision I make."

- **Mini-Challenge:**

Rewrite one fear-based belief into an empowering belief.
Example:

  - **Fear Thought:** "I'm not good enough."
  - **New Thought:** "I am constantly learning and improving."
  - **Fear Thought:**_____
  - **New Thought:**_____

- **Meditation Moment:**

(Picture yourself acting boldly and fearlessly in a situation you've been afraid of.)

Day 5: Taking the First Step Past Fear

- **Today's Reflection Prompt:**

"What small action can I take today to prove to myself that I am stronger than my fear?"

....

....

- **Today's Affirmation:**

"Every step I take weakens fear's hold on me."

- **Mini-Challenge:**
  Do one thing today that challenges your fear, even if it's small.
  Example: Start a conversation, send an email, apply for a job, take a class.

Day 6: Weekly Reflection & Milestone Celebration

- **Today's Reflection Prompt:**
  "What is one major realization I had about fear this week?"

....

....

- **Today's Affirmation:**
  "I am stronger than my fears, and I prove it every day."

- **Milestone Celebration:**
  Write down one fear-based belief you let go of this week.

....

- **Community Connection (Optional but Encouraged):**
  Who can I share this insight with? _____

Week 1 Summary:

- **The fear that has held me back the most is:**

....

....

....

....

- **One limiting belief I rewrote:**

....

....

....

....

- **One action I took despite fear:**

....

....

....

....

Preparing for Next Week:

You are breaking the cycle of fear and self-doubt.

Next, we'll focus on **building self-trust, courage, and confidence to replace fear.**

Fear is just a thought. Your courage is real. Keep moving forward.

Week 2: Overcoming the Fear of Failure (Section 2.2)

Weekly Focus:
Failure is one of the most **deeply ingrained fears** that hold people back. But here's the truth: **Failure isn't the opposite of success—it's part of the process.**

This week, you'll learn how to **reframe failure as a stepping stone, not a stopping point.** You'll build the resilience to **try, fail, and try again—until success becomes inevitable.**

Remember:
Failure is a lesson, not a life sentence.

Monica Lewinsky **once believed her failures defined her.** The entire world judged her for mistakes she made when she was just starting out in life. But she **reclaimed her narrative** and proved that **one failure does not define your future.**

This week, you'll start seeing failure **as fuel for your success.**

Day 7: Defining What Failure Means to You

- **Today's Reflection Prompt:**

"What does failure mean to me? Have I let it define me in the past?"

....

....

- **Today's Affirmation:**

  "Failure is just feedback—it does not define me."

- **Mini-Challenge:**

  Write down one past failure that shaped you and list one positive lesson you gained from it.

....

....

- **Daily Tracker:**

  | Failure Identified ☐ | Lesson Learned ☐ | Journal Completed ☐ |

- **Meditation Moment (2–3 min):**

  Breathe deeply and remind yourself: "Every failure brings me closer to success."
  ☐ Completed Meditation

Day 8: Understanding the Fear of Judgment

- **Today's Reflection Prompt:**

  "Am I more afraid of failing or of what people will think if I fail?"

....

....

- **Today's Affirmation:**

  "Other people's opinions do not define my success."

- **Mini-Challenge:**

  Write down one thing you have avoided because of the fear of judgment.

- **Meditation Moment:**

  (Visualize yourself taking action without worrying about what others think.)

Day 9: The Growth Mindset – Seeing Failure as Learning

- **Today's Reflection Prompt:**

  "What would I try if I knew failure was just part of the learning process?"

....

....

- **Today's Affirmation:**

  "Every mistake is a lesson that makes me stronger."

- **Mini-Challenge:**

  Write down one thing you've been afraid to try because of fear of failure.

....

- **Daily Tracker:**

  | Fear-Based Limitation Identified ☐ | Growth Mindset Applied ☐ | Journal Completed ☐ |

Day 10: Taking Action Despite Fear

- **Today's Reflection Prompt:**

  "What is one small action I can take today to move past my fear of failure?"

....

....

- **Today's Affirmation:**

  "I take action even when I feel fear."

- **Mini-Challenge:**

  Take one step today toward something that scares you.

  Example: Apply for the job, start the project, reach out for help.

- **Meditation Moment:**

  (Picture yourself acting confidently, despite uncertainty.)

Day 11: Reframing Setbacks as Setups for Success

- **Today's Reflection Prompt:**

  "What is one failure I can now see as a setup for success?"

....

....

- **Today's Affirmation:**

  "Every setback is preparing me for something greater."

- **Mini-Challenge:**

  Write down one past failure and reframe it as a setback that led to something better.

  Example: Losing a job → Led me to a better career path.

....

....

- **Daily Tracker:**

  |Failure Reframed☐ |Affirmation Recited☐ |Journal Completed☐ |

Day 12: Weekly Reflection & Milestone Celebration

- **Today's Reflection Prompt:**

  "How has my perspective on failure changed this week?"

....

....

- **Today's Affirmation:**

  "I am no longer afraid of failure—I embrace it as part of success."

- **Milestone Celebration:**

  Write down one fear of failure you let go of this week.

....

- **Community Connection (Optional but Encouraged):**

  Who can I share this insight with? _____

Week 2 Summary:

- **One failure I now see as a lesson:**

....

....

....

....

- **One action I took despite fear:**

....

....

....

- **One way I have redefined failure for myself:**

....

....

....

Preparing for Next Week:

You are shifting your relationship with failure and self-doubt.

Next, we'll focus on destroying the fear of success, so that you can stop playing small in life.

Fear will no longer hold you back—your resilience will push you forward.

Week 3: Destroying the Fear of Success (Section 3.3)

Weekly Focus:

Most people understand the fear of **failure**, but what about the fear of **success**?

If you've ever found yourself **sabotaging opportunities, avoiding risks even when they could lead to something great, or feeling unworthy of success,** you might be holding yourself back not because you're afraid to fail—**but because you're afraid to succeed.**

This week, you'll identify and **destroy the hidden fear of success** that keeps you from **fully stepping into your potential.**

Remember:
Success brings responsibility. When you eliminate fear, you open the door to unlimited possibilities. Monica Lewinsky could have let **fear of public perception and judgment keep her small.** Instead, she took control of her story, stepping into a **new level of success she once feared.**

This week, you'll do the same.

Day 13: Identifying Your Fear of Success

- **Today's Reflection Prompt:**
  "What scares me about success? Do I worry about responsibility, change, or expectations?"

  ....

  ....

- **Today's Affirmation:**
  "I am ready to step into the success I deserve."

- **Mini-Challenge:**
  Write down one way you've held yourself back from success.

  ....

- **Daily Tracker:**
  | Fear of Success Identified ☐ | Affirmation Recited ☐ | Journal Completed ☐ |

- **Meditation Moment (2–3 min):**
  Breathe deeply and remind yourself: "I am capable of handling success."
  ☐ Completed Meditation

Day 14: Unpacking the Fear of Change

- **Today's Reflection Prompt:**
  "What changes would success bring to my life? Am I afraid of those changes?"

  ....

- **Today's Affirmation:**

"I embrace change as a sign of growth and expansion."

- **Mini-Challenge:**

Write down one positive change success would bring into your life.

- **Meditation Moment:**

(Visualize yourself adapting smoothly to change.)

Day 15: Letting Go of Guilt & Self-Sabotage

- **Today's Reflection Prompt:**

"Do I feel guilty about succeeding? Have I ever sabotaged my progress?"

- **Today's Affirmation:**

"I deserve success, and I will not hold myself back."

- **Mini-Challenge:**

Write down one way you can allow yourself to succeed without guilt.

Example: I will remind myself that my success inspires others.

- **Daily Tracker:**

| Guilt Released ☐ | Affirmation Recited ☐ | Journal Completed ☐ |

Day 16: Overcoming the Fear of Standing Out

- **Today's Reflection Prompt:**

"Do I fear attention, leadership, or visibility? Why?"

- **Today's Affirmation:**

  "I am worthy of being seen and recognized for my success."

- **Mini-Challenge:**

  Take one small step today that allows you to be seen.

  Example: Speak up in a meeting, post a win on social media, or share your story with someone.

- **Meditation Moment:**

  (Picture yourself being recognized and respected for your success.)

Day 17: Accepting Success as Your New Normal

- **Today's Reflection Prompt:**

  "What if success wasn't a rare event, but my new reality?"

....

....

- **Today's Affirmation:**

  "Success is a natural part of my life, and I embrace it fully."

- **Mini-Challenge:**

  Write a "Success Statement" that describes yourself as someone who naturally succeeds.

  Example: "I am a person who consistently takes action, achieves my goals, and inspires others."

....
....

- **Meditation Moment:**

  (Visualize yourself feeling completely comfortable with success.)

Day 18: Weekly Reflection & Milestone Celebration

- **Today's Reflection Prompt:**

  "How has my fear of success changed this week?"

....

- **Today's Affirmation:**

  "I welcome success into my life with confidence and ease."

- **Milestone Celebration:**

  Write down one success-based fear you let go of this week.

- **Community Connection (Optional but Encouraged):**

  Who can I share my progress with? _____

Week 3 Summary:

- **One fear of success I identified:**

....

....

....

....

- **One way I embraced change this week:**

....

....

....

- **One small success I allowed myself to celebrate:**

....

....

....

Preparing for Next Week:

You are no longer afraid of failure—or success.

Next, we'll focus on **building resilience and self-trust, so you never question your ability again.**

You don't just deserve success—you are ready for it.

Week 4: Eliminating Self-Doubt Once and For All (Section 3.4)

Weekly Focus:

You've already broken free from **fear of failure and fear of success**, but there's one last major obstacle to confidence: **self-doubt.**

Self-doubt is the **inner voice that questions your ability, worth, and potential.** It makes you hesitate when you should take action, **second-guess your progress,** and hold back when you should be moving forward.

This week, you will learn how to **silence self-doubt permanently** and **replace it with unshakable confidence and self-trust.**

Remember:

You don't have to "feel" confident to take action—confidence is built by taking action despite doubt.

Monica Lewinsky spent years battling **shame, imposter syndrome, and self-doubt.** But instead of letting those thoughts control her, she challenged them, **redefined her self-worth, and rebuilt her confidence step by step.**

This week, you'll do the same.

Day 19: Identifying Your Self-Doubt Triggers

- **Today's Reflection Prompt:**
  "When does my self-doubt show up the most? What situations trigger it?"

- **Today's Affirmation:**
  "I am capable, strong, and fully deserving of success."

- **Mini-Challenge:**
  Identify one specific situation where self-doubt tends to appear and write down how you will challenge it.
  Example:

  - **Trigger:** Public speaking → Challenge: Remind myself that I am prepared and knowledgeable.
  - **Trigger:**_____ → Challenge:_____

- **Daily Tracker:**
  | Self-Doubt Trigger Identified ☐ | Affirmation Recited ☐ | Journal Completed ☐ |

- **Meditation Moment (2–3 min):**
  Breathe deeply and visualize yourself handling a challenging situation with total confidence.
  ☐ Completed Meditation

Day 20: Challenging Negative Self-Talk

- **Today's Reflection Prompt:**
  "What are the most common negative thoughts I tell myself? Are they really true?"

....

....

- **Today's Affirmation:**
  "My thoughts do not control me—I choose empowering beliefs."

- **Mini-Challenge:**
  Write down one self-doubting thought and replace it with a more powerful belief.
  Example:

  - **Self-Doubt:** "I'm not smart enough."
  - **New Thought:** "I am constantly learning and growing."
  - **Self-Doubt:**_____
  - **New Thought:**_____

- **Meditation Moment:**

  (Picture yourself rejecting self-doubt and replacing it with self-belief.)

Day 21: Strengthening Self-Trust

- **Today's Reflection Prompt:**

  "When have I proven to myself that I am strong and capable?"

....

....

- **Today's Affirmation:**

  "I trust myself to handle anything that comes my way."

- **Mini-Challenge:**

  Write down one past moment where you succeeded despite self-doubt.

....

- **Daily Tracker:**

  | Self-Trust Reinforced ☐ | Affirmation Recited ☐ | Journal Completed ☐ |

Day 22: Taking Confident Action Even When You Don't Feel Ready

- **Today's Reflection Prompt:**

  "What is one thing I've been holding back on because of self-doubt?"

....

....

- **Today's Affirmation:**

  "I take action, even when self-doubt tries to hold me back."

- **Mini-Challenge:**

  Do one thing today that you've been avoiding because of self-doubt.

  Example: Apply for a job, reach out to a mentor, start a project.

- **Meditation Moment:**

  (Picture yourself moving through self-doubt with ease, taking bold action.)

Day 23: Practicing Radical Self-Compassion

- **Today's Reflection Prompt:**
  "Am I too hard on myself? How can I show myself more kindness?"

....

....

- **Today's Affirmation:**
  "I am worthy of kindness, patience, and self-love."

- **Mini-Challenge:**
  Write down one way you will be kinder to yourself moving forward.
  Example: I will celebrate progress, not just perfection.

....

....

- **Daily Tracker:**
  | Self-Compassion Practiced ☐ | Affirmation Recited ☐ | Journal Completed ☐ |

Day 24: Weekly Reflection & Milestone Celebration

- **Today's Reflection Prompt:**
  "What is one way I proved to myself that I am stronger than self-doubt this week?"

....

....

- **Today's Affirmation:**
  "I believe in myself fully, and nothing can shake that belief."

- **Milestone Celebration:**
  Write down one self-doubt you eliminated this week.

....

....

- **Community Connection (Optional but Encouraged):**
  Who can I share my progress with? _____

Week 4 Summary:

- **One self-doubt trigger I identified and challenged:**

....

....

....

....

- **One way I replaced self-doubt with self-trust:**

....

....

....

....

- **One action I took despite feeling unsure:**

....

....

....

....

Preparing for Next Week:

You are no longer ruled by self-doubt.

Next, we'll focus on turning your new mindset into lasting confidence and charisma.

You don't need anyone's permission to be confident—you just need to trust yourself.

Week 5: The Action Plan – Face and Conquer Fear Daily (Section 3.5)

Weekly Focus:

Now that you've uncovered the roots of **fear, self-doubt, and limiting beliefs,** it's time to **apply everything you've learned.**

Success isn't about never feeling fear—it's about **taking action despite it.**

This week, you'll follow a **structured plan to face fear daily, strengthen your confidence, and make courage a habit.**

Remember:

Confidence is built through action, not overthinking. The more you practice facing fear, the less power it has over you.

Monica Lewinsky **didn't wake up one day free from fear.** She built confidence **one choice, one action, one bold step at a time**—until fear no longer controlled her.

This week, you will do the same.

Day 25: Define Your Fear-Facing Identity

- **Today's Reflection Prompt:**
  "Who am I when I am fearless? What does my most confident self look like?"

....

....

- **Today's Affirmation:**
  "I am bold, resilient, and unshaken by fear."

- **Mini-Challenge:**
  Write a "Fearless Identity Statement" that describes your strongest, most courageous self.

  Example: "I am someone who takes action despite fear, speaks my truth, and trusts my strength."

....

....

- **Daily Tracker:**
  | Identity Statement Written ☐ | Affirmation Recited ☐ | Journal Completed ☐ |

- **Meditation Moment (2–3 min):**
  Breathe deeply and visualize yourself embodying your fearless identity.
  ☐ Completed Meditation

Day 26: Creating a Daily Courage Ritual

- **Today's Reflection Prompt:**
  "How can I remind myself daily to act with courage?"

....

....

- **Today's Affirmation:**
  "I choose courage as my default setting."

- **Mini-Challenge:**
  Design a Daily Courage Ritual—a simple action that reminds you to face fear.

  Example:

  - **Start each morning by saying:** "What is one brave thing I can do today?"
- **Meditation Moment:**
  (Picture yourself confidently stepping into every new day with purpose.)

Day 27: Taking Small Acts of Courage Every Day

- **Today's Reflection Prompt:**
  "What small action can I take today that pushes me out of my comfort zone?"

....

....

- **Today's Affirmation:**
  "Every day, I take one step that expands my comfort zone."

- **Mini-Challenge:**
  Identify one small action you can take today that challenges fear.
  Example: Speak up in a meeting, introduce yourself to someone new, try something unfamiliar.

- **Daily Tracker:**
  | Courageous Action Taken ☐ | Affirmation Recited ☐ | Journal Completed ☐ |

Day 28: Reframing Fear as Excitement

- **Today's Reflection Prompt:**
  "What if fear and excitement were the same feeling? How would I act differently?"

....

....

- **Today's Affirmation:**
  "Fear is just energy—I choose to turn it into excitement."

- **Mini-Challenge:**
  The next time you feel fear, pause and reframe it as excitement.
  Example:

  - **Instead of "I'm nervous about this opportunity," say:** "I'm excited to grow from this experience."

- **Meditation Moment:**
  (Visualize transforming fear into excitement and motivation.)

Day 29: Reflecting on Your Fear-Facing Wins

- **Today's Reflection Prompt:**
  "What fears have I faced head-on in the last 30 days? How have I grown?"

....

....

- **Today's Affirmation:**
  "I am fearless because I choose courage every day."

- **Mini-Challenge:**
  Write down three moments from the past month when you acted despite fear.

  1. _____

2. _____

3. _____

- **Daily Tracker:**

  | Fear-Facing Reflection Completed ☐ | Affirmation Recited ☐ | Journal Completed ☐ |

Day 30: Celebration & Commitment to Lifelong Courage

- **Today's Reflection Prompt:**

  "How will I continue to face fear and build confidence for life?"

  ....

  ....

- **Today's Affirmation:**

  "I am committed to living boldly and fearlessly."

- **Final Mini-Challenge:**

  Write a letter to your future self, describing what you've learned, how you feel, and your commitment to facing fear daily. (Space at back of this workbook.)

- **Milestone Celebration:**

  Write down one major fear you've overcome in the last 30 days.

  ....

  ....

- **Community Connection (Optional but Encouraged):**

  Who can I share my growth with? _____

Week 5 Summary: (Final Check-In)

- **The biggest fear I conquered this month:**

  ....

  ....

  ....

....

- **My new fearless identity statement:**

....

....

....

....

- **One action I will continue doing daily to keep fear from holding me back:**

....

....

....

....

You've just completed a **30-day journey in overcoming fear and self-doubt,** and in doing so, you've proven something powerful:

Fear is not an immovable force.
Self-doubt is not your identity.
You are stronger than the thoughts that once held you back.

Over the past five weeks, you have:

- Identified and confronted the root of your fears.
- Overcome the fear of failure and the fear of success.
- Rewired your self-image to eliminate self-doubt.
- Built daily habits that reinforce courage and confidence.

But while you've worked hard to **change your mindset,** there's another factor that impacts your success: **your environment.**

Even the strongest mindset can be tested when surrounded by **toxic people, negative influences, or environments that keep you stuck in old patterns.**

Monica Lewinsky reclaimed her narrative and confidence—but only after stepping away from **shame, negativity, and toxic public scrutiny.** She had to **break free from the story others wrote for her** and create her own.

Now, it's time for you to do the same.

In **Chapter 4,** you'll learn how to **identify toxic relationships, break free from unhealthy patterns, and design an environment that supports your transformation.**

You've changed your mind—now it's time to change your surroundings.

Let's begin.

Breaking Free from Toxic Patterns and Negative Environments

You are not obligated to remain in spaces that do not nurture your growth.

Your mindset is powerful, but even the strongest mindset can be weakened by the wrong environment.

Toxic people, negative spaces, and unhealthy patterns can drain your energy, distort your self-worth, and keep you trapped in cycles you've worked so hard to break.

This chapter is about **cutting ties with the habits, people, and environments that no longer serve you—** not out of anger, but out of self-respect.

Few people understand this struggle more than **Susan Burton.** After experiencing profound personal loss and being caught in a cycle of addiction and incarceration, she found herself repeatedly **pulled back into toxic environments** that made change feel impossible. But the moment she made the decision to break free from the **places, influences, and thought patterns that kept her stuck,** she was able to **rebuild her life, reclaim her power, and help others do the same.**

This chapter will guide you in:

- Recognizing toxic people, habits, and spaces that drain your energy.
- Developing the courage to walk away from relationships that hold you back.
- Creating an environment that supports your transformation.
- Designing a life where you no longer feel trapped by your past.

You've changed your mindset—now it's time to change your surroundings.

Let's start by identifying the people and influences that drain you.

Week 1: Identifying Toxic People and Energy Drainers (Section 4.1)

Weekly Focus:
You cannot **heal, grow, or thrive** in the same toxic environments that kept you stuck. The first step to breaking free is **recognizing the people, habits, and spaces that drain your energy—** and understanding that **you have the power to walk away.**

Remember:

Not everyone deserves access to your energy. Protect it wisely.

Day 1: Recognizing Toxic People in Your Life

- **Today's Reflection Prompt:**
  "Who in my life consistently drains my energy, disrespects my boundaries, or makes me feel unworthy?"

....

....

- **Today's Affirmation:**
  "I deserve relationships that uplift and empower me."

- **Mini-Challenge:**
  Write down the names of three people who bring negativity into your life and one way they impact you.

  1. _____

  2. _____

  3. _____

- **Daily Tracker:**
  | Toxic Influence Identified ☐ | Affirmation Recited ☐ | Journal Completed ☐ |

- **Meditation Moment (2–3 min):**
  Breathe deeply and remind yourself: "I have the power to choose who I allow into my life."
  ☐ Completed Meditation

Day 2: Spotting Manipulative and Controlling Behavior

- **Today's Reflection Prompt:**
  "Have I ever felt pressured, manipulated, or controlled in my relationships? What signs did I ignore?"

....

- **Today's Affirmation:**

  "I trust my instincts and remove myself from harmful situations."

- **Mini-Challenge:**

  Write down three warning signs of toxic behavior you will no longer ignore.

- **Meditation Moment:**

  (Picture yourself confidently walking away from situations that do not serve you.)

Day 3: Noticing Emotional Vampires and Energy Drainers

- **Today's Reflection Prompt:**

  "Who or what leaves me feeling emotionally exhausted, even when I try to stay positive?"

- **Today's Affirmation:**

  "I release people and habits that drain my energy."

- **Mini-Challenge:**

  Identify one way you can set a boundary today to protect your energy.

- **Daily Tracker:**

  | Energy Drainer Identified ☐ | Affirmation Recited ☐ | Journal Completed ☐ |

Day 4: Understanding When Loyalty Becomes a Trap

- **Today's Reflection Prompt:**

  "Have I stayed in toxic relationships out of guilt, obligation, or fear?"

....

....

- **Today's Affirmation:**
  "I release guilt and allow myself to grow beyond my past."

- **Mini-Challenge:**
  Write down one relationship or commitment you've outgrown but struggle to walk away from.

....

....

- **Meditation Moment:**
  (Visualize yourself letting go of unhealthy attachments without guilt.)

Day 5: Recognizing How Your Environment Shapes You

- **Today's Reflection Prompt:**
  "Do the places I spend my time in help me grow, or do they pull me backward?"

....

....

- **Today's Affirmation:**
  "I choose to be in environments that nourish and support me."

- **Mini-Challenge:**
  Make a list of three places you spend the most time in and evaluate whether they are helping or hurting you.

  1. _____

  2. _____

  3. _____

- **Daily Tracker:**
  | Environment Evaluated ☐ | Affirmation Recited ☐ | Journal Completed ☐ |

Day 6: Weekly Reflection & Milestone Celebration

- **Today's Reflection Prompt:**
  "What toxic influence have I identified this week that I am ready to release?"

....

....

- **Today's Affirmation:**
  "I am creating space for healthier relationships and environments."

- **Milestone Celebration:**
  Write down one decision you are making to protect your energy moving forward.

....

....

- **Community Connection (Optional but Encouraged):**
  Who can I share my progress with? _____

Week 1 Summary:

- **One toxic relationship or habit I identified:**

....

....

....

....

- **One way I will start protecting my energy:**

....

....

....

....

....

- **One environment I need to change to support my growth:**

....

....

....

....

Preparing for Next Week:

You are no longer allowing toxic influences to drain you.

Next, we'll focus on **identifying and letting go of the destructive habits that have kept you stuck in the past.**

Letting go is not weakness—it's self-respect. Keep choosing yourself.

Week 2: Releasing Old, Destructive Habits (Section 4.2)

Weekly Focus:

Your environment isn't just about **who you surround yourself with**—it's also about **what you repeatedly do.**

Old habits are **powerful anchors** that can keep you stuck in toxic cycles, even when your mind is ready to move forward.

This week, you'll focus on **identifying and breaking free from destructive habits** that hold you back—whether they are thought patterns, behaviors, or routines that no longer serve you.

Remember:

You don't break bad habits by willpower alone—you replace them with habits that support your growth.

Susan Burton **couldn't move forward until she changed her daily routines, her thought patterns, and her reactions to stress.** The moment she made **new, empowering habits part of her daily life,** everything began to change.

This week, you will do the same.

Day 7: Identifying the Habits That Hold You Back

- **Today's Reflection Prompt:**
  "What daily or weekly habits keep me in the same cycle? How do they impact my growth?"

....

....

- **Today's Affirmation:**
  "I release habits that no longer serve me."

- **Mini-Challenge:**
  Write down three destructive habits that have held you back.

....

....

- **Daily Tracker:**
  | Habit Identified ☐ | Affirmation Recited ☐ | Journal Completed ☐ |

- **Meditation Moment (2–3 min):**
  Breathe deeply and remind yourself: "I have the power to change my habits and my life."
  ☐ Completed Meditation

❀ Day 8: Understanding Why Destructive Habits Stick

- **Today's Reflection Prompt:**
  "When do I feel most tempted to fall back into old habits? What triggers them?"

....

....

- **Today's Affirmation:**
  "I recognize my triggers and take control of my actions."

- **Mini-Challenge:**
  Identify one habit trigger and write down a new response you will practice instead.
  Example:

- **Trigger:** Stress → New Response: Take deep breaths instead of reaching for a distraction.
- **Trigger:**_____ → New Response:_____

- **Meditation Moment:**
  (Visualize yourself responding to a trigger in a new, healthy way.)

Day 9: Replacing Old Habits with Empowering Ones

- **Today's Reflection Prompt:**
  "What positive habit can I replace a destructive habit with?"

....

....

- **Today's Affirmation:**
  "I replace old patterns with habits that empower me."

- **Mini-Challenge:**
  Choose one small habit swap to start today.
  Example: Instead of checking social media in the morning, read or stretch for five minutes.

- **Daily Tracker:**
  | Old Habit Replaced ☐ | Affirmation Recited ☐ | Journal Completed ☐ |

- **Meditation Moment:**
  (Picture yourself easily choosing a new habit that supports your growth.)

Day 10: Learning to Navigate Setbacks

- **Today's Reflection Prompt:**
  "How do I usually react when I slip back into old habits? How can I respond with resilience?"

....

....

- **Today's Affirmation:**
  "A setback is not failure—it's an opportunity to learn and grow."

- **Mini-Challenge:**
  Write down one way you will show yourself grace when facing setbacks.

- **Meditation Moment:**
  (Visualize yourself quickly recovering from setbacks without self-judgment.)

Day 11: Creating a Routine That Supports Growth

- **Today's Reflection Prompt:**
  "What daily routine would help me stay consistent in my growth?"

....

....

- **Today's Affirmation:**
  "I create a lifestyle that supports my success."

- **Mini-Challenge:**
  Write out a simple morning or evening routine that reinforces your new habits.

....

....

- **Daily Tracker:**
  | Routine Designed ☐ | Affirmation Recited ☐ | Journal Completed ☐ |

- **Meditation Moment:**
  (Picture yourself effortlessly following your new routine each day.)

Day 12: Weekly Reflection & Milestone Celebration

- **Today's Reflection Prompt:**
  "What is one old habit I have successfully disrupted this week?"

....

....

- **Today's Affirmation:**

"I am in control of my choices, and I choose growth."

- **Milestone Celebration:**
  Write down one major mindset or habit shift from this week.

....

....

- **Community Connection (Optional but Encouraged):**
  Who can I share this progress with? _____

Week 2 Summary:

- **One habit I identified as destructive:**

....

....

....

....

- **One new habit I am choosing instead:**

....

....

....

....

- **One way I will handle setbacks with resilience:**

....

....

....

....

Preparing for Next Week:

You are no longer controlled by old patterns.

Next, we'll focus on **creating positive environments that are optimized for growth.**

You are in control of your choices, your routines, and your future. Keep building the life you deserve.

Week 3: Creating a Positive and Growth-Oriented Environment (Section 4.3)

Weekly Focus:

A toxic environment will **undo progress faster than any setback.** No matter how strong your mindset is, **your surroundings influence your habits, your emotions, and your future.**

The good news? **You don't have to stay stuck in environments that drain you.**

This week, you'll take intentional steps to **build a space—physically, mentally, and socially—that supports your growth.**

Remember:
Your environment should reflect the life you are building, not the one you are leaving behind.

Susan Burton d**idn't just walk away from toxic influences—she built a completely new environment for herself and others.** She **surrounded herself with people who supported her transformation,** created spaces where she could thrive, and eventually **helped others do the same.**

This week, you'll do the same.

Day 13: Identifying What a Growth-Oriented Environment Looks Like for You

- **Today's Reflection Prompt:**
  "What kind of environment helps me feel safe, motivated, and supported?"

....

....

- **Today's Affirmation:**
  "I deserve a space that supports my growth and well-being."

- **Mini-Challenge:**
  Describe your ideal environment—what people, spaces, and habits contribute to it?

  ....

  ....

- **Daily Tracker:**
  | Growth Environment Defined ☐ | Affirmation Recited ☐ | Journal Completed ☐ |

- **Meditation Moment (2–3 min):**
  Breathe deeply and visualize yourself surrounded by an uplifting and supportive space.
  ☐ Completed Meditation

Day 14: Evaluating Your Current Environment

- **Today's Reflection Prompt:**
  "Does my current environment help or hinder my progress? What needs to change?"

  ....

  ....

- **Today's Affirmation:**
  "I have the power to change my surroundings and create a better life."

- **Mini-Challenge:**
  Write down three aspects of your current environment that may be holding you back.

  ....

  ....

- **Meditation Moment:**
  (Picture yourself removing negative elements from your space, making room for growth.)

Day 15: Decluttering and Detoxing Your Space

- **Today's Reflection Prompt:**

"What physical space in my life needs cleansing or organizing?"

....

....

- **Today's Affirmation:**
  "A clear space creates a clear mind."

- **Mini-Challenge:**
  Choose one area of your home or workspace to clean, organize, or refresh today.

- **Daily Tracker:**
  | Space Decluttered ☐ | Affirmation Recited ☐ | Journal Completed ☐ |

- **Meditation Moment:**
  (Imagine yourself feeling lighter and more in control after clearing space in your life.)

Day 16: Curating the Right People in Your Life

- **Today's Reflection Prompt:**
  "Who are the people in my life that truly uplift and support me?"

....

....

- **Today's Affirmation:**
  "I surround myself with people who encourage and inspire me."

- **Mini-Challenge:**
  Write down three people who add value to your life and how you can strengthen those relationships.

  1. _____

  2. _____

  3. _____

- **Meditation Moment:**
  (Picture yourself surrounded by a circle of people who truly support your success.)

Day 17: Setting Boundaries to Protect Your Energy

- **Today's Reflection Prompt:**
  "What boundaries do I need to set to maintain a positive environment?"

....

....

- **Today's Affirmation:**
  "I set clear boundaries that honor my growth and well-being."

- **Mini-Challenge:**
  Write out one boundary you will enforce starting today.
  Example: Limiting time around negative conversations or people.

....

....

- **Daily Tracker:**
  | Boundary Identified ☐ | Affirmation Recited ☐ | Journal Completed ☐ |

- **Meditation Moment:**
  (Visualize yourself setting a firm, respectful boundary and feeling empowered by it.)

Day 18: Weekly Reflection & Milestone Celebration

- **Today's Reflection Prompt:**
  "What is one improvement I made to my environment this week?"

....

....

- **Today's Affirmation:**
  "I am creating a space where I can thrive."

- **Milestone Celebration:**
  Write down one decision you made this week to protect your environment and energy.

....

- **Community Connection (Optional but Encouraged):**
  Who can I share my progress with? _____

Week 3 Summary:

- **One area of my environment I improved:**

....

....

....

....

- **One positive person I want to keep close:**

....

....

....

....

- **One boundary I am enforcing to protect my energy:**

....

....

....

....

Preparing for Next Week:

You are no longer trapped by negative environments—you are designing a life that supports you.

Next, we'll focus on **protecting your energy by setting appropriate boundaries.**

Your environment is your foundation. Keep building one that lifts you higher.

Week 4: Setting Boundaries and Protecting Your Energy (Section 4.4)

Weekly Focus:

You've made incredible progress in **identifying toxic people, breaking free from destructive habits, and creating a growth-oriented environment.** Now, it's time to **set strong boundaries to protect the space you've worked so hard to create.**

Setting boundaries is not about **cutting people off carelessly**—it's about **honoring your growth and choosing peace over chaos.**

Remember:

Your time, energy, and peace are valuable. You don't owe access to everyone.

Susan Burton **had to set clear boundaries to protect her new life.** She knew that without them, she could easily be pulled back into the same cycles she worked so hard to escape.

This week, you'll do the same.

Day 19: Understanding What Boundaries Are and Why They Matter

- **Today's Reflection Prompt:**
  "Have I ever felt exhausted, used, or taken advantage of? What situations led to those feelings?"

....

....

- **Today's Affirmation:**
  "I have the right to protect my time, energy, and peace."

- **Mini-Challenge:**
  Write down one past situation where a lack of boundaries caused stress or burnout.

....

....

- **Daily Tracker:**
  | Boundary Awareness Gained ☐ | Affirmation Recited ☐ | Journal Completed ☐ |

- **Meditation Moment (2–3 min):**

Breathe deeply and remind yourself: "My boundaries are a sign of self-respect."
☐ Completed Meditation

Day 20: Identifying Where You Need Stronger Boundaries

- **Today's Reflection Prompt:**

"Where in my life do I need stronger boundaries? (Work, relationships, family, friendships, social media, etc.)"

....

....

- **Today's Affirmation:**

"I set clear, healthy boundaries that honor my well-being."

- **Mini-Challenge:**

Choose one area of your life where you need a stronger boundary and describe what that boundary will look like.

....

....

- **Meditation Moment:**

(Visualize yourself setting boundaries with confidence and clarity.)

Day 21: Communicating Boundaries with Confidence

- **Today's Reflection Prompt:**

"What makes me hesitant to set boundaries? Am I afraid of conflict, rejection, or guilt?"

....

....

- **Today's Affirmation:**

"I communicate my needs clearly, without guilt or fear."

- **Mini-Challenge:**
  Write a boundary statement you can use in real-life situations.
  Example: "I can't take on extra work this weekend—I need time for myself."

....

....

- **Daily Tracker:**
  | Boundary Statement Created ☐ | Affirmation Recited ☐ | Journal Completed ☐ |

- **Meditation Moment:**
  (Picture yourself confidently stating your boundary to someone who respects it.)

Day 22: Enforcing Boundaries and Handling Pushback

- **Today's Reflection Prompt:**
  "What will I do when someone ignores or pushes back against my boundaries?"

....

....

- **Today's Affirmation:**
  "I stand firm in my boundaries, even when challenged."

- **Mini-Challenge:**
  Write down one way you will reinforce a boundary if someone tests it.
  Example: If someone keeps overstepping, I will politely remind them of my boundary and follow through with consequences.

- **Meditation Moment:**
  (Visualize yourself standing strong in your boundaries, free from guilt.)

Day 23: Setting Boundaries with Yourself

- **Today's Reflection Prompt:**
  "What personal boundaries do I need to set for myself? (Time management, self-discipline, emotional regulation, social media use, etc.)"

....

....

- **Today's Affirmation:**
"I honor my own boundaries as much as I honor those with others."

- **Mini-Challenge:**
Choose one self-boundary to set and commit to following it.
Example: I will not check my phone first thing in the morning—I will start my day with intention.

- **Daily Tracker:**
| Self-Boundary Set ☐ | Affirmation Recited ☐ | Journal Completed ☐ |

- **Meditation Moment:**
(Picture yourself respecting your personal limits and feeling in control.)

Day 24: Weekly Reflection & Milestone Celebration

- **Today's Reflection Prompt:**
"What is one boundary I set this week that made a difference in my peace and well-being?"

....

....

- **Today's Affirmation:**
"I protect my energy, time, and mental space with confidence."

- **Milestone Celebration:**
Write down one decision you made this week to enforce a boundary successfully.

....

....

- **Community Connection (Optional but Encouraged):**
Who can I share my progress with? _____

Week 4 Summary:

- **One area where I needed stronger boundaries:**

....

....

....

....

- **One boundary I successfully communicated this week:**

....

....

....

....

- **One way I will continue protecting my energy moving forward:**

....

....

....

....

Preparing for Next Week:

You have the power to create and enforce boundaries that protect your well-being.

Next, we'll focus on **fully cutting ties with toxic influences and relationships that no longer serve you.**

Boundaries are an act of self-love—honor them, and you will thrive.

Week 5: The Action Plan – Detox Your Life for Success (Section 4.5)

Weekly Focus:

You've done the deep work to **identify toxic people, break destructive habits, create a growth-oriented** environment, and set boundaries—now it's time to take **full control of your life** and detox anything that doesn't align with your success.

This final week is all about **action**. You'll systematically remove **negative influences, distractions, and toxic cycles** while reinforcing **the habits, relationships, and spaces that empower you.**

Remember:
When you remove what no longer serves you, you make space for what truly helps you grow.

Susan Burton **didn't just hope for change—she took bold steps to detox her life completely.** She **let go of toxic influences, built a foundation of discipline and support, and committed to an environment that matched her new vision.**

This week, you'll do the same.

Day 25: Conducting a Life Detox Audit

- **Today's Reflection Prompt:**
  "What areas of my life still feel toxic or out of alignment with my growth?"

....

....

- **Today's Affirmation:**
  "I release everything that no longer serves my highest good."

- **Mini-Challenge:**
  Make a "Toxicity Audit" List by writing down anything—habits, people, behaviors, places, or mindsets—that no longer align with your future.

....

....

- **Daily Tracker:**
  | Life Detox Audit Completed ☐ | Affirmation Recited ☐ | Journal Completed ☐ |

- **Meditation Moment (2–3 min):**
  Breathe deeply and visualize yourself removing these toxic influences from your life.
  ☐ Completed Meditation

Day 26: Cutting Ties with One Toxic Influence

- **Today's Reflection Prompt:**
  "What or who do I need to distance myself from to protect my energy?"

....

....

- **Today's Affirmation:**
  "I am strong enough to walk away from what holds me back."

- **Mini-Challenge:**
  Choose one toxic relationship, habit, or environment to cut off or reduce your exposure to—then take one concrete step today toward releasing it.

- **Daily Tracker:**
  | Toxic Influence Released ☐ | Affirmation Recited ☐ | Journal Completed ☐ |

- **Meditation Moment:**
  (Picture yourself feeling lighter and freer after cutting this toxic tie.)

Day 27: Decluttering Your Physical and Digital Space

- **Today's Reflection Prompt:**
  "Does my physical or digital space support the person I'm becoming?"

....

....

- **Today's Affirmation:**
  "I create an environment that reflects my growth and success."

- **Mini-Challenge:**
  Choose one area to declutter today—your home, workspace, phone, social media, or schedule.

- **Daily Tracker:**
  | Space Decluttered ☐ | Affirmation Recited ☐ | Journal Completed ☐ |

- **Meditation Moment:**

(Visualize your space as clean, organized, and free from unnecessary distractions.)

Day 28: Strengthening Your Support System

- **Today's Reflection Prompt:**
  "Who are the people I want to keep close because they uplift and support me?"

....

....

- **Today's Affirmation:**
  "I surround myself with people who inspire and challenge me to grow."

- **Mini-Challenge:**
  Reach out to one positive person in your life today—send a message, make a call, or plan time together.

- **Daily Tracker:**
  | Positive Connection Strengthened ☐ | Affirmation Recited ☐ | Journal Completed ☐ |

- **Meditation Moment:**
  (Visualize yourself surrounded by a strong, positive support system.)

Day 29: Creating a Long-Term Detox Plan

- **Today's Reflection Prompt:**
  "What systems can I put in place to make sure I don't fall back into toxic patterns?"

....

....

- **Today's Affirmation:**
  "I am committed to protecting my peace and my future."

- **Mini-Challenge:**
  Write down three strategies to maintain your detox long-term.
  Example: Setting monthly check-ins with yourself, surrounding yourself with accountability partners, or tracking progress in a journal.

....

....

- **Daily Tracker:**
  | Long-Term Detox Plan Created ☐ | Affirmation Recited ☐ | Journal Completed ☐ |

- **Meditation Moment:**
  (Picture yourself living free from toxic influences, fully in control of your life.)

Day 30: Celebration & Commitment to a Toxic-Free Life

- **Today's Reflection Prompt:**
  "What is the biggest change I have made in the past 30 days?"

....

- **Today's Affirmation:**
  "I am free from toxic patterns, and I choose growth every day."

- **Final Mini-Challenge:**
  Write a letter to your future self about your transformation and commitment to protecting your peace. (Space at back of this workbook.)

- **Milestone Celebration:**
  Write down one major toxic influence you have successfully removed from your life.

....

....

- **Community Connection (Optional but Encouraged):**
  Who can I share my growth with? _____

Week 5 Summary: (Final Check-In)

- **One major toxic influence I removed from my life:**

....

....

....

....

- **One system I will use to maintain my detox long-term:**

....

....

....

- **One way I will protect my energy moving forward:**

....

....

....

You've just completed a **30-day journey of detoxing your life for success,** and in doing so, you've made one of the most powerful choices a person can make: **choosing yourself.**

You've taken the hard but necessary steps to:

- Identify and release toxic people, habits, and environments.
- Create boundaries that protect your energy and well-being.
- Design a life that nurtures your growth, not drains it.
- Fully commit to maintaining a life free from negativity and toxicity.

But **clearing out toxic influences is just the first step.** Now, it's time to **fill that space with discipline, focus, and productivity** so you can actively build the future you deserve.

Susan Burton's journey didn't end when she **removed toxic patterns and environments—it truly began when she developed the discipline to stay on her new path, take control of her habits, and work toward something greater.**

In **Chapter 5**, you'll learn how to:

- Develop self-discipline that lasts, even when motivation fades.
- Take control of your time and energy for maximum productivity.
- Replace procrastination with action and momentum.
- Build daily habits that turn success into a natural, automatic process.

You've removed what was holding you back—now it's time to build what will move you forward.

Let's begin.

Chapter 5

Mastering Self-Discipline and Unstoppable Productivity

Motivation gets you started. Discipline keeps you going.

Most people wait for **motivation** to strike before taking action. But if you've learned anything from the journey so far, it's that **waiting for motivation is a trap**—because motivation comes and goes.

What **truly separates those who succeed from those who stay stuck is self-discipline.**

Self-discipline is the ability to take consistent action, even when you don't feel like it. It's about making the choice—**day after day, moment after moment**—to push forward despite discomfort, boredom, or resistance.

No one knows this better than Marchell Taylor.

After spending **25 years incarcerated,** Marchell was released with no money, no job, and a past that could have easily kept him stuck. But instead of making excuses, he made a plan. **He built self-discipline from the ground up, committed to daily progress, and used his time wisely.** He created a strict schedule for himself, never wasted a moment, and developed the habits that would ultimately turn him into a successful entrepreneur and mentor.

Marchell didn't wait for inspiration—**he built his future through self-discipline.**

In this chapter, you will learn how to:

- Understand the science behind self-discipline and how to strengthen it like a muscle.
- Create habits that make discipline automatic.
- Overcome procrastination, distractions, and time-wasters.
- Build a personal system for unstoppable productivity.

You've cleared space for growth. Now it's time to take control of your habits, your time, and your future.

Let's start with understanding the **science behind self-discipline**—and how you can train your brain to become unstoppable.

Week 1: The Science Behind Self-Discipline (Section 5.1)

Weekly Focus:

Self-discipline isn't something you either **have or don't have**—it's something you **train**.

Your brain is wired to seek **comfort and short-term pleasure**, which is why discipline feels hard at first. But the good news? **You can reprogram your brain** to crave progress instead of procrastination.

This week, you'll learn how **discipline works on a neurological level**, and how to **train yourself to take action automatically, without overthinking.**

Remember:

Discipline is a skill—not a personality trait. The more you practice it, the stronger it becomes.

Day 1: Understanding How Self-Discipline Works

- **Today's Reflection Prompt:**
  "Do I rely on motivation, or do I have systems that keep me disciplined?"

....

....

- **Today's Affirmation:**
  "I build my discipline daily, and it gets stronger every time I use it."

- **Mini-Challenge:**
  Identify one area of your life where you struggle with discipline.
  Example: Waking up early, sticking to a routine, staying focused.

- **Daily Tracker:**
  | Discipline Challenge Identified ☐ | Affirmation Recited ☐ | Journal Completed ☐ |

- **Meditation Moment (2–3 min):**
  Breathe deeply and visualize yourself effortlessly following through on your commitments.
  ☐ Completed Meditation

Day 2: Strengthening Your Self-Discipline Muscle

- **Today's Reflection Prompt:**

"What small action can I take today to strengthen my discipline?"

....

....

- **Today's Affirmation:**
"Self-discipline is a muscle, and I make it stronger every day."

- **Mini-Challenge:**
Choose one small task that you will commit to every day this week, no matter what.
Example: Drink a glass of water every morning, make your bed, journal for 2 minutes.

- **Daily Tracker:**
| Daily Discipline Task Chosen ☐ | Affirmation Recited ☐ | Journal Completed ☐ |

- **Meditation Moment:**
(Visualize yourself completing your daily discipline habit effortlessly.)

Day 3: The Power of Delayed Gratification

- **Today's Reflection Prompt:**
"What is one area where I tend to seek instant gratification instead of long-term success?"

....

....

- **Today's Affirmation:**
"I choose long-term success over short-term comfort."

- **Mini-Challenge:**
Identify one thing you will delay or resist today in favor of long-term benefits.
Example: Avoid social media until after completing a task, skip an impulse purchase, choose a workout over TV.

- **Daily Tracker:**
| Delayed Gratification Challenge Completed ☐ | Affirmation Recited ☐ | Journal Completed ☐ |

- **Meditation Moment:**
(Picture yourself making choices that serve your future instead of seeking quick pleasure.)

Day 4: Overcoming Resistance and Mental Blocks

- **Today's Reflection Prompt:**
"What excuse do I tell myself when I don't feel like being disciplined?"

....

....

- **Today's Affirmation:**
"I take action, even when I don't feel like it."

- **Mini-Challenge:**
The next time you feel resistance, count down from 5 and take immediate action.
Example: 5…4…3…2…1—start your workout, begin your task, get out of bed.

- **Daily Tracker:**
| Resistance Challenge Completed ☐ | Affirmation Recited ☐ | Journal Completed ☐ |

- **Meditation Moment:**
(Visualize yourself acting immediately, without hesitation.)

Day 5: Training Your Brain to Love Discipline

- **Today's Reflection Prompt:**
"What if self-discipline became enjoyable instead of a struggle?"

....

....

- **Today's Affirmation:**
"I find joy and satisfaction in my discipline."

- **Mini-Challenge:**
Make one disciplined action feel rewarding today—play music while working, reward yourself after completing a task, or focus on how good progress feels.

- **Daily Tracker:**
| Enjoyable Discipline Task Completed ☐ | Affirmation Recited ☐ | Journal Completed ☐ |

- **Meditation Moment:**
  (Picture yourself enjoying the feeling of self-discipline and progress.)

Day 6: Weekly Reflection & Milestone Celebration

- **Today's Reflection Prompt:**
  "How has my understanding of self-discipline changed this week?"

....

....

- **Today's Affirmation:**
  "I am becoming more disciplined every single day."

- **Milestone Celebration:**
  Write down one disciplined action you completed consistently this week.

....

....

- **Community Connection (Optional but Encouraged):**
  Who can I share my progress with? _____

Week 1 Summary:

- **One way I trained my discipline this week:**

....

....

....

....

- **One area where I delayed gratification successfully:**

....

....

....

....

- **One way I will continue strengthening my self-discipline muscle:**

....

....

....

....

Preparing for Next Week:

You now understand that self-discipline is a skill you can train and improve.

Next, we'll focus on **destroying procrastination by creating habits that make discipline automatic and effortless.**

Discipline isn't about forcing yourself—it's about becoming the type of person who follows through, no matter what.

Week 2: Destroying Procrastination and Taking Massive Action (Section 5.2)

Weekly Focus:

If self-discipline is the foundation of success, then **procrastination is its biggest enemy.**

Procrastination **steals time, kills momentum, and keeps you stuck in a cycle of delay, regret, and unfinished goals.**

The truth? **Procrastination isn't about laziness—it's about fear, overwhelm, and a lack of structure.**

This week, you'll uncover the **root causes of your procrastination** and learn **how to take immediate, massive action**—no more waiting, no more excuses.

Remember:

The fastest way to build confidence and success is to take action—before you feel ready.

Marchell Taylor didn't have **time to procrastinate.** He spent **25 years behind bars,** and when he was released, he knew every moment mattered. Instead of waiting for the perfect time or ideal conditions, **he took immediate action every single day.**

He didn't wait for motivation—**he created momentum.**

This week, you'll do the same.

Day 7: Understanding Why You Procrastinate

- **Today's Reflection Prompt:**
  "What tasks do I avoid the most, and why?"

....

....

- **Today's Affirmation:**
  "I face challenges head-on instead of avoiding them."

- **Mini-Challenge:**
  Write down one task you've been avoiding and why you think you keep putting it off.

....

....

- **Daily Tracker:**
  | Procrastination Trigger Identified ☐ | Affirmation Recited ☐ | Journal Completed ☐ |

- **Meditation Moment (2–3 min):**
  Breathe deeply and remind yourself: "Taking action now is always easier than delaying it."
  ☐ Completed Meditation

Day 8: Breaking the Cycle of Overthinking

- **Today's Reflection Prompt:**
  "How often do I spend more time thinking about a task than actually doing it?"

....

....

- **Today's Affirmation:**

  "I act quickly and decisively—progress matters more than perfection."

- **Mini-Challenge:**

  The next time you catch yourself overthinking, count down from 5 and take action immediately.

- **Daily Tracker:**

  | Overthinking Challenge Completed ☐ | Affirmation Recited ☐ | Journal Completed ☐ |

- **Meditation Moment:**

  (Visualize yourself breaking free from hesitation and jumping into action.)

Day 9: The 2-Minute Rule – Taking Immediate Action

- **Today's Reflection Prompt:**

  "What small task can I complete immediately instead of postponing it?"

  ....

  ....

- **Today's Affirmation:**

  "I take action now—no matter how small."

- **Mini-Challenge:**

  Apply the 2-minute rule: If something takes less than two minutes, do it now.
  Example: Respond to an email, wash a dish, organize your workspace.

- **Daily Tracker:**

  | 2-Minute Task Completed ☐ | Affirmation Recited ☐ | Journal Completed ☐ |

- **Meditation Moment:**

  (Picture yourself instantly completing small tasks without hesitation.)

Day 10: Tackling the Biggest Task First

- **Today's Reflection Prompt:**

  "What is the most important task I've been avoiding?"

- **Today's Affirmation:**

  "I do the hardest task first and gain momentum for the rest of the day."

- **Mini-Challenge:**

  Apply the Eat the Frog Method—do your hardest task first thing in the morning.

- **Daily Tracker:**

  | Hardest Task Completed First ☐ | Affirmation Recited ☐ | Journal Completed ☐ |

- **Meditation Moment:**

  (Visualize the feeling of relief and accomplishment after completing a major task.)

Day 11: Building Momentum Through Small Wins

- **Today's Reflection Prompt:**

  "What small win can I create today that will build momentum?"

- **Today's Affirmation:**

  "Small wins lead to massive success."

- **Mini-Challenge:**

  Choose one small, easy task to complete first thing in the morning to create momentum.
  Example: Make your bed, do 10 push-ups, send an email.

- **Daily Tracker:**

  | Small Win Completed ☐ | Affirmation Recited ☐ | Journal Completed ☐ |

- **Meditation Moment:**

  (Picture your small win leading to bigger successes throughout the day.)

Day 12: Weekly Reflection & Milestone Celebration

- **Today's Reflection Prompt:**
  "How has taking immediate action changed my productivity this week?"

....

....

- **Today's Affirmation:**
  "I am becoming an action-taker—my success is in my hands."

- **Milestone Celebration:**
  Write down one major thing you accomplished this week by taking action instead of procrastinating.

....

....

- **Community Connection (Optional but Encouraged):**
  Who can I share my progress with? _____

Week 2 Summary:

- **One procrastination habit I broke:**

....

....

....

....

- **One major task I completed instead of avoiding:**

....

....

....

....

- **One strategy I will continue using to take immediate action:**

....

....

....

....

Preparing for Next Week:

You now understand how to stop procrastinating and take action immediately.

Next, we'll focus on **mastering time management and eliminating distractions for unstoppable productivity.**

Success isn't about doing more—it's about doing the right things, at the right time, with full focus.

Week 3: Developing Laser-Focused Productivity (Section 5.3)

Weekly Focus:
You've learned how to s**top procrastination and take massive action**—now, it's time to **maximize your focus and efficiency.**

The most successful people aren't the ones who do the most. **They're the ones who focus on the right things and execute them with precision.**

This week, you'll learn how to:

- Manage your time like a high performer.
- Eliminate distractions that sabotage your focus.
- Train your brain for deep work and sustained productivity.
- Make every hour count without burning out.

Remember:
Focus isn't about doing more—it's about doing what truly matters, with full attention.

Marchell Taylor didn't just work hard—**he worked smart.** He had to maximize every moment to rebuild his life. He learned to **cut out distractions, prioritize his time, and focus deeply on what moved him forward.**

This week, you'll do the same.

Day 13: Understanding the Power of Deep Work

- **Today's Reflection Prompt:**

"How often do I truly focus without distractions? How does my work quality change when I do?"

- **Today's Affirmation:**

"When I focus deeply, I produce my best work."

- **Mini-Challenge:**

Set a 30-minute Deep Work Session today. Pick one important task and eliminate all distractions while working on it.

- **Daily Tracker:**

| Deep Work Session Completed ☐ | Affirmation Recited ☐ | Journal Completed ☐ |

- **Meditation Moment (2–3 min):**

Breathe deeply and remind yourself: "My focus is my superpower."
☐ Completed Meditation

Day 14: Identifying Your Biggest Time Wasters

- **Today's Reflection Prompt:**

"What distractions steal my time the most? (Phone, social media, emails, unnecessary tasks, etc.)"

- **Today's Affirmation:**

"I take control of my time and eliminate distractions."

- **Mini-Challenge:**

Track how much time you spend on distractions today. Be honest with yourself.

- **Daily Tracker:**

| Time-Wasting Activity Identified ☐ | Affirmation Recited ☐ | Journal Completed ☐ |

- **Meditation Moment:**
  (Visualize yourself easily ignoring distractions and staying locked into your work.)

Day 15: Using the Pomodoro Technique for Peak Focus

- **Today's Reflection Prompt:**
  "How can I structure my work to improve my focus and efficiency?"

....

....

- **Today's Affirmation:**
  "I work with purpose and stay fully engaged."

- **Mini-Challenge:**
  Try the Pomodoro Technique: Work for 25 minutes, take a 5-minute break, then repeat.

- **Daily Tracker:**
  | Pomodoro Session Completed ☐ | Affirmation Recited ☐ | Journal Completed ☐ |

- **Meditation Moment:**
  (Picture yourself completing tasks with focus, energy, and efficiency.)

Day 16: Eliminating Decision Fatigue

- **Today's Reflection Prompt:**
  "What decisions do I make daily that drain my mental energy?"

....

....

- **Today's Affirmation:**
  "I simplify my life and focus only on what matters."

- **Mini-Challenge:**
  Reduce one unnecessary decision by creating a system.
  Example: Plan your outfit the night before, set a meal prep routine, or automate a task.

- **Daily Tracker:**
  | Decision Fatigue Reduced ☐ | Affirmation Recited ☐ | Journal Completed ☐ |

- **Meditation Moment:**
  (Visualize your day flowing effortlessly because of smart decisions.)

Day 17: Creating a Distraction-Free Zone

- **Today's Reflection Prompt:**
  "What in my environment disrupts my focus, and how can I change it?"

....

....

- **Today's Affirmation:**
  "I design my space for focus, success, and productivity."

- **Mini-Challenge:**
  Optimize your workspace by removing one distraction or adding an element that helps you focus (e.g., noise-canceling headphones, clean workspace, better lighting).

- **Daily Tracker:**
  | Distraction-Free Zone Created ☐ | Affirmation Recited ☐ | Journal Completed ☐ |

- **Meditation Moment:**
  (Picture yourself working in a peaceful, focused environment.)

Day 18: Weekly Reflection & Milestone Celebration

- **Today's Reflection Prompt:**
  "What was my biggest breakthrough in focus and productivity this week?"

....

....

- **Today's Affirmation:**
  "I use my time wisely and work with full focus."

- **Milestone Celebration:**
  Write down one major task you completed this week because of improved focus.

  ....

  ....

- **Community Connection (Optional but Encouraged):**
  Who can I share my progress with? _____

Week 3 Summary:

- **One major distraction I eliminated:**

  ....

  ....

  ....

  ....

- **One productivity technique that worked for me:**

  ....

  ....

  ....

- **One way I will continue improving my focus:**

  ....

  ....

  ....

Preparing for Next Week:

You've mastered deep focus—now, let's turn your productivity into a powerful system.

Next, we'll explore **how a well-structured morning routine can set the tone for your entire day and increase your focus and energy.**

High achievers don't just work harder—they work smarter. Let's build a system that works for you.

Week 4: Building a Bulletproof Morning Routine (Section 5.4)

Weekly Focus:
The way you **start your day** determines how you **spend your day.**

Highly successful people don't just wake up and **hope for a productive day**—they have a **structured morning routine** that sets them up for success.

Your morning habits are the foundation of **your discipline, focus, and energy levels.** If you win the morning, you win the day.

Remember:
Your first hour shapes the next 23. Make it count.

Marchell Taylor understood the power of **structure and consistency.** While incarcerated, he developed **strict daily routines** that helped him **build discipline, self-respect, and a sense of control over his future.**

After his release, he carried that same **morning structure into his new life,** using it to build success **one day at a time.**

This week, you'll do the same by designing and committing to a **morning routine that fuels your success.**

Day 19: Designing Your Ideal Morning Routine

- **Today's Reflection Prompt:**
  "If I could create the perfect morning routine, what would it look like?"

....

....

- **Today's Affirmation:**
  "My mornings set the tone for a powerful and productive day."

- **Mini-Challenge:**
  Write down three key habits you want in your morning routine.
  Example: Stretching, reading, meditation, hydration, journaling, goal-setting.

  1. _____

  2. _____

  3. _____

- **Daily Tracker:**
  | Morning Routine Designed ☐ | Affirmation Recited ☐ | Journal Completed ☐ |

- **Meditation Moment (2–3 min):**
  Breathe deeply and visualize yourself waking up with energy, clarity, and purpose.
  ☐ Completed Meditation

Day 20: Waking Up with Intention

- **Today's Reflection Prompt:**
  "Do I wake up with purpose, or do I hit snooze and rush through my mornings?"

....

....

- **Today's Affirmation:**
  "I wake up with clarity, energy, and purpose."

- **Mini-Challenge:**
  Set your alarm 30 minutes earlier than usual and use that time for a morning habit.

- **Daily Tracker:**
  | Intentional Wake-Up Time Set ☐ | Affirmation Recited ☐ | Journal Completed ☐ |

- **Meditation Moment:**
  (Visualize yourself waking up excited to start your day.)

Day 21: Mastering the First 10 Minutes of Your Day

- **Today's Reflection Prompt:**

  "How do I currently spend my first 10 minutes of the day? Is it helping or hurting me?"

  ....

  ....

- **Today's Affirmation:**

  "I control how my day starts, and I choose success."

- **Mini-Challenge:**

  Design a 10-minute morning ritual that gets you in the right mindset.

  Example: Drink water, stretch, deep breathing, express gratitude, or set intentions.

- **Daily Tracker:**

  | 10-Minute Ritual Practiced ☐ | Affirmation Recited ☐ | Journal Completed ☐ |

- **Meditation Moment:**

  (Picture yourself beginning each morning with purpose and clarity.)

Day 22: Fueling Your Body and Mind for Success

- **Today's Reflection Prompt:**

  "What is one healthy habit I can add to my morning that fuels my energy?"

  ....

  ....

- **Today's Affirmation:**

  "I nourish my body and mind with healthy morning habits."

- **Mini-Challenge:**

  Add one health-focused habit to your morning routine.

  Example: Drink water, eat a nutritious breakfast, exercise, or journal.

- **Daily Tracker:**

  | Health Habit Added ☐ | Affirmation Recited ☐ | Journal Completed ☐ |

- **Meditation Moment:**

  (Visualize yourself feeling strong, energized, and ready to conquer the day.)

Day 23: Eliminating Morning Distractions

- **Today's Reflection Prompt:**

  "What distractions ruin my morning momentum, and how can I remove them?"

....

....

- **Today's Affirmation:**

  "I protect my mornings from distractions and stay focused on my goals."

- **Mini-Challenge:**

  Choose one morning distraction to eliminate this week.

  Example: Avoid checking your phone first thing in the morning.

- **Daily Tracker:**

  | Morning Distraction Eliminated ☐ | Affirmation Recited ☐ | Journal Completed ☐ |

- **Meditation Moment:**

  (Picture yourself starting your morning without distractions, fully in control of your time.)

Day 24: Weekly Reflection & Milestone Celebration

- **Today's Reflection Prompt:**

  "How has my morning routine improved my focus and discipline this week?"

....

....

- **Today's Affirmation:**

  "My mornings belong to me, and I use them to create success."

- **Milestone Celebration:**

  Write down one habit you have successfully built into your morning routine.

....

....

- **Community Connection (Optional but Encouraged):**
  Who can I share my progress with? _____

Week 4 Summary:

- **One change I made to my morning routine:**

....

....

....

....

- **One distraction I eliminated:**

....

....

....

....

- **One way my mornings are making me more productive:**

....

....

....

....

Preparing for Next Week:

You now have a morning routine that sets you up for success.

Next, we'll focus on **creating a personalized system to maintain discipline and productivity long-term.**

Routines build discipline. Discipline builds success. Keep refining your mornings until they work for you.

Week 5: The Action Plan – Daily Self-Discipline Blueprint (Section 5.5)

Weekly Focus:

Self-discipline is the foundation of **every success you will ever achieve.** You've spent the past four weeks **strengthening your discipline muscle, eliminating distractions, and designing a productive life—** now, it's time to **lock it in as a permanent way of living.**

This final week is about **creating a system that makes discipline automatic.** No more relying on motivation. No more struggling with procrastination.

You're building a **bulletproof system** that ensures you **stay on track no matter what.**

Remember:
Discipline is doing what needs to be done, even when you don't feel like it.

Marchell Taylor didn't just develop discipline while incarcerated—**he carried it into his new life and used it to build his future.** His success wasn't based on luck or talent—it was built through **consistent, disciplined action every single day.**

This week, you'll do the same.

Day 25: Creating Your Non-Negotiable Daily Habits

- **Today's Reflection Prompt:**
  "What daily habits are essential for my growth and success?"

....

....

- **Today's Affirmation:**
  "I commit to the habits that bring me closer to my goals."

- **Mini-Challenge:**

Choose three non-negotiable daily habits that you will follow every day, no matter what.
Example: Wake up early, read for 10 minutes, exercise, journal, meditate, plan your day.

....

....

- **Daily Tracker:**
  | Non-Negotiable Habits Set ☐ | Affirmation Recited ☐ | Journal Completed ☐ |

- **Meditation Moment (2–3 min):**
  Breathe deeply and visualize yourself following your habits effortlessly.
  ☐ Completed Meditation

Day 26: The Power of Planning Your Day in Advance

- **Today's Reflection Prompt:**
  "Do I start my day with a clear plan, or do I let the day control me?"

....

....

- **Today's Affirmation:**
  "I plan my day with intention and execute with purpose."

- **Mini-Challenge:**
  Plan tomorrow's schedule before going to bed tonight.
  Example: Block time for priorities, set a clear morning routine, list three must-do tasks.

- **Daily Tracker:**
  | Daily Plan Created ☐ | Affirmation Recited ☐ | Journal Completed ☐ |

- **Meditation Moment:**
  (Visualize yourself waking up with a plan and executing it flawlessly.)

Day 27: Tracking Your Progress and Holding Yourself Accountable

- **Today's Reflection Prompt:**
  "How can I measure my progress and keep myself accountable?"

....

....

- **Today's Affirmation:**

  "I track my progress and stay committed to my goals."

- **Mini-Challenge:**

  Create a daily habit tracker or journal to track your progress.

  Example: Use a simple checklist or app to log habits.

- **Daily Tracker:**

  | Habit Tracking System Created ☐ | Affirmation Recited ☐ | Journal Completed ☐ |

- **Meditation Moment:**

  (Picture yourself staying consistent and seeing real progress over time.)

Day 28: Setting Boundaries to Protect Your Time and Focus

- **Today's Reflection Prompt:**

  "What time-wasters or distractions do I need to eliminate from my daily routine?"

....

....

- **Today's Affirmation:**

  "I protect my time and energy by setting clear boundaries."

- **Mini-Challenge:**

  Set one boundary that protects your time and discipline.

  Example: No phone in the first hour of the morning, no unnecessary meetings, time limits on social media.

- **Daily Tracker:**

  | Boundary Implemented ☐ | Affirmation Recited ☐ | Journal Completed ☐ |

- **Meditation Moment:**

  (Visualize yourself setting strong boundaries and sticking to them with confidence.)

Day 29: Creating a Fail-Proof System for Discipline

- **Today's Reflection Prompt:**
  "What systems can I put in place to make self-discipline easier?"

....

....

- **Today's Affirmation:**
  "I create systems that make discipline effortless."

- **Mini-Challenge:**
  Automate or structure one aspect of your daily discipline to reduce friction.
  Example: Meal prep to avoid unhealthy eating, set reminders for habits, prep your workout gear the night before.

- **Daily Tracker:**
  | Discipline System Created ☐ | Affirmation Recited ☐ | Journal Completed ☐ |

- **Meditation Moment:**
  (Picture your self-discipline running on autopilot, making success inevitable.)

Day 30: Celebration & Commitment to Lifelong Discipline

- **Today's Reflection Prompt:**
  "How has self-discipline transformed my life over the past 30 days?"

....

....

- **Today's Affirmation:**
  "Self-discipline is who I am. I control my habits, my time, and my success."

- **Final Mini-Challenge:**
  Write a letter to your future self, committing to maintaining your self-discipline for life. (Space at back of this workbook.)

- **Milestone Celebration:**
  Write down one major transformation you've achieved through discipline.

  ....

  ....

- **Community Connection (Optional but Encouraged):**
  Who can I share my growth with? _____

Week 5 Summary: (Final Check-In)

- **One discipline habit I've built for life:**

  ....

  ....

  ....

  ....

- **One system I've created to maintain my productivity:**

  ....

  ....

  ....

- **One way I will hold myself accountable going forward:**

  ....

  ....

  ....

  ....

You've just completed a **30-day journey in mastering self-discipline and unstoppable productivity,** and in doing so, you've proven that **your success is in your control.**

Over the past five weeks, you have:
- Strengthened your self-discipline like a muscle.
- Destroyed procrastination and built a bias for action.
- Developed laser-focused productivity and deep work habits.
- Created a morning routine that fuels success.
- Designed a personal system that makes discipline automatic.

Discipline doesn't just shape your **habits and productivity**—it shapes **your entire future.** Now, it's time to **apply that same discipline to your financial success.**

Money is one of the biggest sources of **stress, struggle, and limitation** for many people—but it doesn't have to be. By developing a w**ealth mindset, taking control of your finances, and making strategic moves**, you can **break free from scarcity and build true financial stability.**

Marchell Taylor didn't just rebuild his life through discipline—he used it to c**hange his relationship with money, create opportunities, and secure his future.**

In Chapter 6, you'll learn how to:

- Develop a wealth mindset that attracts success.
- Escape financial struggle and build lasting security.
- Make smart money moves, even if you're starting from zero.
- Create financial habits that set you up for lifelong abundance.

You've mastered self-discipline—now, let's apply it to your financial future.

Let's begin.

Chapter 6

Financial Success & Wealth Mindset Transformation

Wealth is not just about money—it's about mindset, strategy, and discipline.

For many people, **money is a source of stress, limitation, or even fear.** Whether you've struggled with financial insecurity, made mistakes with money, or simply never learned how to build wealth, it can feel like financial success is out of reach.

But the truth is, **wealth is not just about how much money you make—it's about how you think, act, and make decisions about money.**

No one understands this better than **Curtis "Wall Street" Carroll.** Incarcerated at 17, Curtis had never even **read a financial statement, let alone thought about building wealth.** But while in prison, he made a life-changing decision—**to educate himself about money, investing, and financial freedom.**

He didn't let his circumstances define him. Instead, he used his time behind bars to master the principles of wealth, apply financial discipline, and create opportunities for himself and others.

Today, Curtis is a **self-taught investor, financial educator, and advocate for financial literacy in underserved communities.** He proves that **it's never too late to change your financial future**—as long as you change your mindset first.

In this chapter, you'll learn how to:

- Understand and shift your money mindset to attract financial success.
- Escape scarcity thinking and build a wealth-oriented mentality.
- Make smart financial moves, even if you're starting with nothing.
- Develop habits that lead to financial security and long-term wealth.

Your financial situation is not set in stone—your mindset and actions will determine your future.

Let's start by uncovering the **beliefs and habits that shape your money mindset.**

Week 1: Understanding Your Money Mindset (Section 6.1)

Weekly Focus:

Your **thoughts, beliefs, and habits around money** shape your financial reality more than your income does.

Some people make millions and **still feel broke**. Others start with nothing and **build lasting wealth**—all because of **how they think and act with money.**

This week, you'll identify **your current money mindset, replace limiting beliefs with wealth-building thoughts, and create a foundation for financial success.**

Remember:

You don't need to be rich to start thinking like a wealthy person. But you do need to think like a wealthy person to become rich.

Curtis "Wall Street" Carroll **realized that financial literacy was his way out of poverty.** Instead of making excuses, he **educated himself, reprogrammed his mindset, and created wealth from the most unlikely place—a prison cell.**

This week, you'll take the first step toward doing the same.

Day 1: Identifying Your Money Beliefs

- **Today's Reflection Prompt:**
  "What beliefs about money did I grow up with? Are they helping or hurting me?"

  ....

  ....

- **Today's Affirmation:**
  "I have the power to rewrite my money story."

- **Mini-Challenge:**
  Write down three beliefs about money you inherited from family, culture, or past experiences.
  Example: "Money is hard to earn," "Rich people are greedy," "I'll never get ahead."

  1. _____

  2. _____

  3. _____

- **Daily Tracker:**
  | Money Belief Identified ☐ | Affirmation Recited ☐ | Journal Completed ☐ |

- **Meditation Moment (2–3 min):**
  Breathe deeply and visualize yourself developing a healthy, empowered relationship with money.
  ☐ Completed Meditation

Day 2: Reframing Scarcity Thinking

- **Today's Reflection Prompt:**
  "Do I operate from a mindset of scarcity (fear, lack) or abundance (opportunity, growth)?"

....

....

- **Today's Affirmation:**
  "Money is a tool, and I have the power to create abundance."

- **Mini-Challenge:**
  Identify one area of your life where scarcity thinking has held you back, and reframe it with an abundance mindset.
  Example: Instead of "I can't afford that," say "How can I create the income to afford that?"

....

....

- **Daily Tracker:**
  | Scarcity Thought Reframed ☐ | Affirmation Recited ☐ | Journal Completed ☐ |

- **Meditation Moment:**
  (Visualize yourself making money decisions from a place of confidence and abundance.)

Day 3: Overcoming Fear of Financial Success

- **Today's Reflection Prompt:**
  "Does the idea of financial success excite me or make me uncomfortable? Why?"

....

- **Today's Affirmation:**
  "I am worthy of financial success and the freedom it brings."

- **Mini-Challenge:**
  Write down one fear or doubt you have about making or managing money, and a strategy to overcome it.
  Example: Fear: "I'm not good with money." → Strategy: "I will educate myself and take control of my finances."

- **Daily Tracker:**
  | Financial Fear Addressed ☐ | Affirmation Recited ☐ | Journal Completed ☐ |

- **Meditation Moment:**
  (Visualize yourself confidently managing wealth and making empowered financial choices.)

Day 4: Breaking the Cycle of Financial Struggle

- **Today's Reflection Prompt:**
  "Have I accepted financial struggle as normal? How can I break that cycle?"

- **Today's Affirmation:**
  "I am breaking the cycle of financial struggle and creating wealth for my future."

- **Mini-Challenge:**
  Write down one financial habit that keeps you stuck, and one action to replace it.
  Example: Habit: Impulse spending → New Action: Track every expense for the next 7 days.

- **Daily Tracker:**
  | Financial Habit Identified ☐ | Affirmation Recited ☐ | Journal Completed ☐ |

- **Meditation Moment:**
  (Picture yourself free from financial stress, making confident money choices.)

Day 5: Creating a Wealth Mindset Mantra

- **Today's Reflection Prompt:**
  "What new belief about money do I want to adopt moving forward?"

....

....

- **Today's Affirmation:**
  "I attract wealth by making smart decisions and taking bold action."

- **Mini-Challenge:**
  Write your personal wealth mantra—a belief about money that will guide your financial decisions.
  Example: "Money flows to me because I use it wisely."

....

....

- **Daily Tracker:**
  | Wealth Mantra Created ☐ | Affirmation Recited ☐ | Journal Completed ☐ |

- **Meditation Moment:**
  (Repeat your wealth mantra and visualize yourself building financial success.)

Day 6: Weekly Reflection & Milestone Celebration

- **Today's Reflection Prompt:**
  "How has my money mindset shifted this week?"

....

....

- **Today's Affirmation:**

  "I am in control of my financial future."

- **Milestone Celebration:**

  Write down one money belief you've changed and how it will impact your life.

....

....

- **Community Connection (Optional but Encouraged):**

  Who can I share my progress with? _____

Week 1 Summary:

- **One money belief I've reprogrammed:**

....

....

....

....

- **One action I'm taking to shift from scarcity to abundance:**

....

....

....

- **One way I will continue strengthening my wealth mindset:**

....

....

....

Preparing for Next Week:

You now have the mindset of someone who builds wealth.

Next, we'll focus on escaping the paycheck-to-paycheck trap through awareness.

Wealth isn't just about money—it's about the habits and decisions that create financial freedom. Keep going.

Week 2: Escaping the Paycheck-to-Paycheck Trap (Section 6.2)

Weekly Focus:

Living paycheck to paycheck **is not just a financial challenge—it's a mental and emotional burden**. The constant stress of wondering if you'll have enough to cover bills, emergencies, and basic needs can keep you trapped in a cycle of survival mode.

But the truth is, **you can break free from this trap.** No matter where you're starting from, small but intentional financial changes can create a **path to financial stability and freedom.**

This week, you'll learn how to:

- Understand why so many people stay stuck in the paycheck-to-paycheck cycle.
- Shift from reactive spending to intentional money management.
- Create breathing room in your finances, even on a limited income.
- Take control of your cash flow so you're no longer just "getting by."

Remember:

You are not meant to just survive—you are meant to thrive.

Curtis "Wall Street" Carroll grew up **believing financial struggle was normal.** But after educating himself, he realized **financial freedom is possible for anyone who learns the right skills and makes smart choices.**

This week, you'll take the first steps toward doing the same.

Day 7: Understanding Why You're Stuck in the Cycle

- **Today's Reflection Prompt:**
  "What are the main reasons I feel stuck living paycheck to paycheck?"

....

....

- **Today's Affirmation:**
  "I am taking control of my financial future."

- **Mini-Challenge:**
  Write down three reasons why you're currently struggling financially.
  Example: High expenses, low income, lack of savings, impulse spending, unexpected costs.

  1. _____

  2. _____

  3. _____

- **Daily Tracker:**
  | Paycheck-to-Paycheck Challenge Identified ☐ | Affirmation Recited ☐ | Journal Completed ☐ |

- **Meditation Moment (2–3 min):**
  Breathe deeply and remind yourself: "I have the power to change my financial situation."
  ☐ Completed Meditation

Day 8: Tracking Where Your Money Is Really Going

- **Today's Reflection Prompt:**
  "Do I truly know where my money goes each month?"

....

....

- **Today's Affirmation:**
  "I am aware of my spending and make intentional financial decisions."

- **Mini-Challenge:**
- Write down every single expense from the past three days—no judgment, just awareness.

....

....

- **Daily Tracker:**
  | Spending Tracked ☐ | Affirmation Recited ☐ | Journal Completed ☐ |

- **Meditation Moment:**
  (Visualize yourself in full control of your money, making informed and empowered choices.)

Day 9: Creating a Simple Budget That Works for You

- **Today's Reflection Prompt:**
  "What can I adjust in my spending to create more financial breathing room?"

- **Today's Affirmation:**
  "I create a budget that supports my goals and my peace of mind."

- **Mini-Challenge:**
  Create a basic budget by categorizing your spending into Needs, Wants, and Savings.
  Example:

  - **Needs:** Rent, food, utilities.
  - **Wants:** Entertainment, dining out, subscriptions.
  - **Savings:** Emergency fund, debt repayment, investments.

- **Daily Tracker:**
  | Budget Created ☐ | Affirmation Recited ☐ | Journal Completed ☐ |

- **Meditation Moment:**
  (Picture yourself following your budget easily and confidently.)

Day 10: Cutting Unnecessary Expenses Without Feeling Deprived

- **Today's Reflection Prompt:**

"What expenses can I reduce or eliminate to gain financial freedom?"

....

....

- **Today's Affirmation:**
  "I prioritize what truly matters and cut what doesn't serve me."

- **Mini-Challenge:**
  Find one expense you can reduce this month and take action today.
  Example: Cancel unused subscriptions, cook at home instead of eating out, switch to a lower phone plan.

- **Daily Tracker:**
  | Expense Cut ☐ | Affirmation Recited ☐ | Journal Completed ☐ |

- **Meditation Moment:**
  (Picture yourself freeing up money for what truly matters in your life.)

Day 11: Increasing Your Income – Small Changes, Big Impact

- **Today's Reflection Prompt:**
  "What are some ways I can increase my income, even in small ways?"

....

....

- **Today's Affirmation:**
  "I am resourceful and capable of creating more financial opportunities."

- **Mini-Challenge:**
  Brainstorm three ways to increase your income and commit to taking action on one.
  Example: Pick up extra shifts, sell unused items, start a side hustle, ask for a raise.

  1. _____

  2. _____

  3. _____

- **Daily Tracker:**
  | Income-Boosting Idea Identified ☐ | Affirmation Recited ☐ | Journal Completed ☐ |

- **Meditation Moment:**
  (Visualize yourself having more financial options and freedom.)

Day 12: Weekly Reflection & Milestone Celebration

- **Today's Reflection Prompt:**
  "What changes have I made this week that give me more financial control?"

  ....

  ....

- **Today's Affirmation:**
  "I am no longer just surviving—I am creating financial freedom."

- **Milestone Celebration:**
  Write down one financial change you've made this week that will help you break the paycheck-to-paycheck cycle.

  ....

  ....

- **Community Connection (Optional but Encouraged):**
  Who can I share my progress with? _____

Week 2 Summary:

- **One spending habit I changed:**

....

....

....

....

- **One unnecessary expense I eliminated:**

....

....

....

....

- **One way I am increasing my income:**

....

....

....

....

Preparing for Next Week:

You now have the foundation to escape the paycheck-to-paycheck cycle.

Next, we'll focus on **adopting new wealthy mindsets by rewiring your brain.**

Your money should work for you—not the other way around. Keep taking control.

Week 3: Rewiring for Wealth and Success (Section 6.3)

Weekly Focus:

Breaking free from financial struggle isn't just about **earning more money**—it's about **thinking differently about money, opportunity, and success.**

Many people stay stuck in financial stress **because they carry limiting beliefs about wealth**. They associate money with greed, guilt, or fear—or they believe they'll never be able to get ahead.

But the truth? **Wealth isn't just for the lucky—it's for those who train their minds for success.**

This week, you'll learn how to:

- Rewire your brain for financial success.
- Adopt the habits and mindset of wealthy individuals.

- Build confidence in managing, growing, and investing money.
- Shift from financial survival to financial power.

Remember:

If you think like a broke person, you'll always be broke. If you think like a wealth-builder, your financial reality will change.

Curtis "Wall Street" Carroll didn't have money, connections, or a financial education growing up. But in prison, he **changed his mindset, studied wealth-building strategies, and trained himself to think like an investor.**

Now, it's your turn to rewire your thinking for financial success.

Day 13: Identifying Your Limiting Beliefs About Money

- **Today's Reflection Prompt:**
  "What negative beliefs about money have I accepted as truth?"

  ....

  ....

- **Today's Affirmation:**
  "I release all limiting beliefs about money and success."

- **Mini-Challenge:**
  Write down three negative beliefs you've held about money and rewrite them with a wealth mindset. Example:

  - **Old Belief:** "I'll never be rich." → New Belief: "Wealth is created through smart decisions and discipline."
  - **Old Belief:** "Rich people are greedy." → New Belief: "Wealth allows me to help others and make a difference."
  - **Old Belief:**_____ → New Belief:_____
  - **Old Belief:**_____ → New Belief:_____
  - **Old Belief:**_____ → New Belief:_____

- **Daily Tracker:**
  | Limiting Belief Rewritten ☐ | Affirmation Recited ☐ | Journal Completed ☐ |

- **Meditation Moment (2–3 min):**
  Breathe deeply and visualize yourself thinking like a wealth-builder, free from fear or doubt.
  ☐ Completed Meditation

Day 14: Adopting a Growth Mindset About Money

- **Today's Reflection Prompt:**
  "Do I see financial success as something I can learn and improve at, or something only a few people achieve?"

....

....

- **Today's Affirmation:**
  "Wealth is a skill I can master with time and effort."

- **Mini-Challenge:**
  Find one resource (book, podcast, video) that teaches financial literacy and commit to learning from it.
  Example: Read a chapter from a personal finance book, listen to a podcast on wealth-building.

- **Daily Tracker:**
  | Financial Learning Completed ☐ | Affirmation Recited ☐ | Journal Completed ☐ |

- **Meditation Moment:**
  (Visualize yourself absorbing financial knowledge and applying it to your life.)

Day 15: Developing a Long-Term Wealth Vision

- **Today's Reflection Prompt:**
  "What kind of financial future do I want for myself and my family?"

....

....

- **Today's Affirmation:**
  "I am building a financial future that supports my goals and dreams."

- **Mini-Challenge:**
  Write down a vision statement for your financial future.
  Example: "I am financially independent, living debt-free, and have multiple streams of income."

....

....

- **Daily Tracker:**
  | Wealth Vision Statement Created ☐ | Affirmation Recited ☐ | Journal Completed ☐ |

- **Meditation Moment:**
  (Picture yourself living in financial freedom, with money working for you instead of against you.)

Day 16: Learning to Make Money Work for You

- **Today's Reflection Prompt:**
  "Am I working for money, or am I making money work for me?"

....

....

- **Today's Affirmation:**
  "I use money wisely to create opportunities and long-term wealth."

- **Mini-Challenge:**
  Research one way to make money work for you instead of just earning and spending it.
  Example: Learn about investing, passive income, or starting a business.

- **Daily Tracker:**
  | Money Strategy Researched ☐ | Affirmation Recited ☐ | Journal Completed ☐ |

- **Meditation Moment:**
  (Visualize yourself in control of your money, making powerful financial decisions.)

Day 17: Taking the First Step Toward Financial Power

- **Today's Reflection Prompt:**
  "What is one financial action I can take today that my future self will thank me for?"

....

....

- **Today's Affirmation:**

  "Every smart financial decision I make today builds my future success."

- **Mini-Challenge:**

  Take one financial action today that moves you toward wealth.

  Example: Open a savings account, start tracking expenses, make an extra debt payment.

- **Daily Tracker:**

  | Wealth-Building Action Taken ☐ | Affirmation Recited ☐ | Journal Completed ☐ |

- **Meditation Moment:**

  (Picture yourself making daily financial choices that lead to long-term success.)

Day 18: Weekly Reflection & Milestone Celebration

- **Today's Reflection Prompt:**

  "What is the biggest shift I've made in my money mindset this week?"

....

....

- **Today's Affirmation:**

  "I am in control of my financial future, and I make smart money decisions daily."

- **Milestone Celebration:**

  Write down one limiting belief you've let go of and one financial goal you're excited to work toward.

- **Community Connection (Optional but Encouraged):**

  Who can I share my progress with? _____

Week 3 Summary:

- **One limiting belief I replaced with a wealth mindset:**

....

....

....

....

- **One way I'm making money work for me instead of just working for money:**

....

....

....

....

- **One financial action I'm committed to taking moving forward:**

....

....

....

....

Preparing for Next Week:

You've rewired your mind for wealth—now, let's create financial security.

Next, we'll focus on **building financial stability, eliminating debt, and creating an emergency fund.**

Wealth starts in the mind—but it becomes real when you take action. Keep moving forward.

Week 4: Taking Control of Your Financial Future (Section 6.4)

Weekly Focus:

Financial success isn't about **luck or waiting for the right opportunity**—it's about **making intentional decisions every day that move you closer to financial freedom.**

Many people feel powerless over their financial situation, but the truth is **you have more control than you**

think. When you take ownership of your money—where it goes, how it's used, and how it grows—you shift from a **passive spender to an active wealth builder.**

This week, you'll learn how to:

- Create a financial plan that supports your long-term success.
- Eliminate debt and build financial stability.
- Develop habits that keep your money working for you.
- Stop reacting to financial stress and start making proactive decisions.

Remember:

You are the CEO of your financial future. It's time to take control.

Curtis "Wall Street" Carroll understood that **no one was coming to save him.** If he wanted financial success, he had to take control of his own future. He studied money, made a plan, and took action **even before he had a dime to invest.**

Now, it's your turn.

Day 19: Creating a Personal Financial Game Plan

- **Today's Reflection Prompt:**
  "What does financial success look like for me? What do I want my money to do for me?"

....

....

- **Today's Affirmation:**
  "I create a financial plan that supports my goals and future."

- **Mini-Challenge:**
  Write out a basic financial game plan with short-term and long-term goals.
  Example:

  - **Short-Term:** Save $500, pay off a small debt, build a budget.
  - **Long-Term:** Become debt-free, build an emergency fund, start investing.
  - **Short-Term:**_____
  - **Long-Term:**_____

- **Daily Tracker:**
  | Financial Game Plan Created ☐ | Affirmation Recited ☐ | Journal Completed ☐ |

- **Meditation Moment (2–3 min):**
  Visualize yourself following a clear financial plan with confidence and clarity.
  ☐ Completed Meditation

Day 20: Eliminating Debt for Good

- **Today's Reflection Prompt:**
  "How does debt affect my financial future? What steps can I take to reduce it?"

....

....

- **Today's Affirmation:**
  "I take control of my debt and create financial freedom."

- **Mini-Challenge:**
  List all your debts (credit cards, loans, etc.) and create a debt elimination plan.
  Example: Use the snowball method (paying off smallest debts first) or the avalanche method (paying off highest-interest debts first).

- **Daily Tracker:**
  | Debt Payoff Plan Created ☐ | Affirmation Recited ☐ | Journal Completed ☐ |

- **Meditation Moment:**
  (Picture yourself free from debt, making empowered financial choices.)

Day 21: Building a Strong Financial Safety Net

- **Today's Reflection Prompt:**
  "What unexpected financial situations have stressed me out in the past?"

....

....

- **Today's Affirmation:**

"I build financial security so I am prepared for anything."

- **Mini-Challenge:**
  Open a separate savings account (if you haven't already) for your emergency fund.
  Goal: Start by saving at least $5–$20 per week.

- **Daily Tracker:**
  | Emergency Fund Started ☐ | Affirmation Recited ☐ | Journal Completed ☐ |

- **Meditation Moment:**
  (Picture yourself financially secure, with money set aside for unexpected expenses.)

Day 22: Automating Your Financial Growth

- **Today's Reflection Prompt:**
  "How can I make good financial decisions automatic?"

....

....

- **Today's Affirmation:**
  "I set up systems that make financial success effortless."

- **Mini-Challenge:**
  Set up one automatic financial habit today.
  Example: Auto-transfer a percentage of your income to savings, automate bill payments, or round up purchases to save extra cash.

- **Daily Tracker:**
  | Financial Automation Set Up ☐ | Affirmation Recited ☐ | Journal Completed ☐ |

- **Meditation Moment:**
  (Visualize money working for you effortlessly, without stress.)

Day 23: Shifting from Spender to Investor

- **Today's Reflection Prompt:**
  "How can I start using my money to build wealth instead of just spending it?"

- **Today's Affirmation:**
  "I make smart financial decisions that create lasting wealth."

- **Mini-Challenge:**
  Research one simple investment option (stocks, real estate, index funds) and write down one step you can take to start investing.

- **Daily Tracker:**
  | Investment Knowledge Gained ☐ | Affirmation Recited ☐ | Journal Completed ☐ |

- **Meditation Moment:**
  (Picture yourself making smart investment decisions and growing your wealth.)

Day 24: Weekly Reflection & Milestone Celebration

- **Today's Reflection Prompt:**
  "What financial changes have I made this week that give me more control over my future?"

- **Today's Affirmation:**
  "I am taking charge of my financial success and building a secure future."

- **Milestone Celebration:**
  Write down one financial decision you made this week that will benefit your future.

- **Community Connection (Optional but Encouraged):**
  Who can I share my progress with? _____

Week 4 Summary:

- **One major financial change I made this week:**

....

....

....

....

- **One financial system I created to make success automatic:**

....

....

....

....

- **One way I will continue growing my financial knowledge:**

....

....

....

....

Preparing for Next Week:

You now have a financial plan, a system for eliminating debt, and a strategy for growing wealth.

Next, we'll map out your **personalized wealth blueprint—ensuring that the habits and strategies you've learned turn into a long-term plan for financial success.**

Financial success is not just about making money—it's about making money work for you. Keep building.

Week 5: The Action Plan – Creating Your Wealth Blueprint (Section 6.5)

Weekly Focus:

Now that you've **transformed your money mindset, escaped financial stress, and built a foundation for stability**, it's time to **create a long-term wealth strategy.**

Wealth isn't built by accident—it's **the result of smart, disciplined actions taken consistently over time.**

This week, you'll create a **personalized wealth blueprint** that outlines:

- Your long-term financial goals.
- The habits and systems that will keep you financially secure.
- How you will grow your income and multiply your wealth.
- A step-by-step plan to build the future you deserve.

Remember:

Financial freedom is not about how much money you make—it's about how well you manage, invest, and grow what you have.

Curtis "Wall Street" Carroll didn't wait until he had money to create his wealth plan—**he created his blueprint first and built his financial future one step at a time.**

Now, it's your turn.

Day 25: Defining Your Wealth Vision

- **Today's Reflection Prompt:**
  "What does financial success mean to me? What kind of lifestyle do I want to create?"

....

....

- **Today's Affirmation:**
  "I define wealth on my own terms and build a future that aligns with my vision."

- **Mini-Challenge:**
  Write out a clear vision for your financial future, including how much you want to earn, save, invest, and the kind of financial security you want.

....

....

....

....

- **Daily Tracker:**
  | Wealth Vision Statement Created ☐ | Affirmation Recited ☐ | Journal Completed ☐ |

- **Meditation Moment (2–3 min):**
  Visualize yourself living in full financial freedom, without stress or limitations.
  ☐ Completed Meditation

Day 26: Automating Wealth-Building Habits

- **Today's Reflection Prompt:**
  "How can I make saving and investing automatic so I never have to rely on willpower?"

....

....

- **Today's Affirmation:**
  "I create financial systems that make wealth-building effortless."

- **Mini-Challenge:**
  Set up one automated financial system today.
  Example: Auto-transfer a percentage of your income to savings or investments, use an app that rounds up spare change for savings.

- **Daily Tracker:**
  | Financial Automation Set Up ☐ | Affirmation Recited ☐ | Journal Completed ☐ |

- **Meditation Moment:**
  (Picture money flowing effortlessly into your savings and investments every month.)

Day 27: Creating Multiple Streams of Income

- **Today's Reflection Prompt:**
  "What are ways I can create additional income to build wealth faster?"

....

....

- **Today's Affirmation:**
  "I attract multiple streams of income that grow my financial future."

- **Mini-Challenge:**
  Brainstorm three ways to create an extra stream of income, and commit to taking the first step toward one of them.
  Example: Start a side hustle, learn about investing, freelance work, rental income, passive income strategies.

  1. _____

  2. _____

  3. _____

- **Daily Tracker:**
  | Income-Boosting Strategy Identified ☐ | Affirmation Recited ☐ | Journal Completed ☐ |

- **Meditation Moment:**
  (Visualize yourself having multiple sources of income, giving you complete financial freedom.)

Day 28: Investing for Long-Term Growth

- **Today's Reflection Prompt:**
  "How can I make my money work for me instead of just working for money?"

....

....

- **Today's Affirmation:**
  "I make wise investments that build long-term financial freedom."

- **Mini-Challenge:**
  Research one simple investment option (stocks, index funds, real estate) and write down one step you can take to start investing.

- **Daily Tracker:**
  | Investment Research Completed ☐ | Affirmation Recited ☐ | Journal Completed ☐ |

- **Meditation Moment:**
  (Picture yourself as a successful investor, making informed and confident financial decisions.)

Day 29: Planning for Generational Wealth

- **Today's Reflection Prompt:**
  "How can I ensure that my financial success benefits future generations?"

....

....

- **Today's Affirmation:**
  "I create wealth that lasts beyond my lifetime."

- **Mini-Challenge:**
  Write down one action you can take to build generational wealth.
  Example: Open a retirement account, create a will, start an investment fund for family, teach financial literacy to loved ones.

....

....

- **Daily Tracker:**
  | Generational Wealth Plan Started ☐ | Affirmation Recited ☐ | Journal Completed ☐ |

- **Meditation Moment:**
  (Visualize your children, family, or future generations benefiting from the wealth you create today.)

Day 30: Celebration & Commitment to Lifelong Wealth-Building

- **Today's Reflection Prompt:**
  "How has my financial mindset and habits transformed over the past 30 days?"

....

- **Today's Affirmation:**
  "I am financially empowered, and I build wealth with confidence."

- **Final Mini-Challenge:**
  Write a letter to your future self, committing to maintaining your wealth-building habits for life.
  (Space at back of this workbook.)

- **Milestone Celebration:**
  Write down one major financial achievement you've made in the past 30 days.

  ....

  ....

- **Community Connection (Optional but Encouraged):**
  Who can I share my progress with? _____

Week 5 Summary: (Final Check-In)

- **One wealth-building habit I've committed to for life:**

....

....

....

....

- **One system I've created to ensure financial security:**

....

....

....

....

- **One financial goal I'm excited to achieve next:**

....

....

....

....

You've just completed a **30-day journey in transforming your financial mindset, escaping financial stress, and building a foundation for lasting wealth.**

Over the past five weeks, you have:

- Rewired your thinking for financial success.
- Broken free from the paycheck-to-paycheck cycle.
- Taken control of your money with strategic habits and systems.
- Created a blueprint for building wealth, growing your income, and securing your future.

But financial success isn't just about numbers—it's about **confidence, self-worth, and the belief that you deserve success.**

Many people struggle with self-doubt, imposter syndrome, and fear of stepping into their full potential. But true wealth—both financial and personal—requires the ability to **own your value, stand strong in your identity, and walk into every situation with confidence.**

Curtis "Wall Street" Carroll didn't just build financial success—he developed **unshakable confidence in his ability to create the life he wanted.** He understood that **confidence is a skill that can be trained, just like financial literacy.**

In **Chapter 7**, you'll learn how to:

- Develop self-confidence that commands respect and opens doors.
- Overcome self-doubt, fear of judgment, and imposter syndrome.
- Master body language, communication, and presence to exude charisma.
- Step into leadership and own your personal power.

You've built financial confidence—now it's time to build the confidence to own every room you walk into.

Let's begin.

Chapter 7

Developing Unshakable Confidence and Charisma

Confidence is not about being perfect—it's about believing in yourself, even when others don't.

Confidence isn't something you're born with—**it's a skill you build.**

Many people believe that confidence is reserved for the naturally outgoing, the successful, or those with an easy path in life. But the truth is, **the most confident people are often those who have struggled the most, failed the hardest, and yet, refused to let their setbacks define them.**

Reginald Dwayne Betts is living proof of this.

At 16, he made a decision that led to his incarceration, and for years, he was labeled **a convicted felon—a statistic, a lost cause.** But instead of allowing his circumstances to define him, he rebuilt himself. **Through reading, writing, and relentless self-improvement, he transformed from an inmate into a Yale-educated lawyer, poet, and advocate for criminal justice reform.**

His confidence wasn't given to him—it was forged through **resilience, knowledge, and the decision to reclaim his identity.**

In this chapter, you'll learn how to:

- Understand the psychology of confidence and how to develop it.
- Overcome fear, self-doubt, and the negative labels of the past.
- Master body language, voice, and communication to exude charisma.
- Step into leadership and develop a presence that commands respect.

Confidence isn't about having no fear—it's about moving forward despite it.

Let's begin by exploring **the psychology behind confidence and how you can start developing it today.**

Week 1: The Psychology of Confidence (Section 7.1)

Weekly Focus:
Confidence isn't about arrogance—it's about **believing in your worth and showing up fully in every situation.**

But for many people, confidence feels out of reach. Years of **self-doubt, negative experiences, and fear of judgment** can make you believe that confidence is something "other people" have.

The truth? **Confidence is a mental habit, a trained skill, and a choice you make every day.**

This week, you'll learn how to:

- Understand the psychology of confidence and what holds you back.
- Challenge limiting beliefs that keep you stuck.
- Reprogram your mind to think and act with confidence.
- Take the first steps toward becoming a more confident version of yourself.

Remember:

Confidence is built, not inherited. And you're about to start building yours.

Reginald Dwayne Betts could have **let society's judgment destroy his self-worth**—but he chose to redefine himself. Confidence was part of his transformation. **Now, it's your turn.**

Day 1: Identifying What's Holding You Back

- **Today's Reflection Prompt:**
  "What experiences or beliefs have made me doubt myself?"

  ....

  ....

- **Today's Affirmation:**
  "My past does not define my confidence—my actions do."

- **Mini-Challenge:**
  Write down one experience that damaged your confidence, and one way you can reframe it.
  Example: "I was told I wasn't good enough." → "That was their opinion, not my truth."

  ....

  ....

- **Daily Tracker:**
  | Confidence Block Identified ☐ | Affirmation Recited ☐ | Journal Completed ☐ |

- **Meditation Moment (2–3 min):**

Breathe deeply and visualize yourself letting go of past doubts and stepping into a confident version of yourself.

☐ Completed Meditation

Day 2: Understanding How Confidence is Built

- **Today's Reflection Prompt:**
  "Do I believe confidence is something I can develop? Why or why not?"

....

....

- **Today's Affirmation:**
  "Confidence is a skill I can strengthen every day."

- **Mini-Challenge:**
  Find a role model (real or historical) who built confidence over time, and write down one lesson you can learn from them.
  Example: Nelson Mandela, Michelle Obama, Malcolm X, Oprah Winfrey.

....

....

- **Daily Tracker:**
  | Confidence Role Model Identified ☐ | Affirmation Recited ☐ | Journal Completed ☐ |

- **Meditation Moment:**
  (Picture yourself growing more confident each day, just like your role model.)

Day 3: Rewiring Your Thoughts for Confidence

- **Today's Reflection Prompt:**
  "What negative self-talk do I catch myself repeating? How can I change it?"

....

....

- **Today's Affirmation:**

"I replace self-doubt with self-belief."

- **Mini-Challenge:**

Write down three negative thoughts you often have about yourself and create a confident response to each.

Example:

  - **Negative Thought:** "I'm not good enough."
  - **Confident Response:** "I am constantly improving and learning."
  - **Negative Thought:**_____
  - **Confident Response:**_____
  - **Negative Thought:**_____
  - **Confident Response:**_____
  - **Negative Thought:**_____
  - **Confident Response:**_____

- **Daily Tracker:**

| Negative Thought Reframed ☐ | Affirmation Recited ☐ | Journal Completed ☐ |

- **Meditation Moment:**

(Visualize yourself speaking to yourself with kindness, confidence, and self-respect.)

Day 4: Overcoming Fear of Judgment

- **Today's Reflection Prompt:**

"How much of my self-doubt comes from worrying about what others think?"

....

....

- **Today's Affirmation:**

"I do not seek approval—I trust myself."

- **Mini-Challenge:**

Do one small thing today without overthinking what others might think.

Example: Wear something bold, share your opinion in a conversation, post a thought online.

- **Daily Tracker:**
  | Fear of Judgment Challenged ☐ | Affirmation Recited ☐ | Journal Completed ☐ |

- **Meditation Moment:**
  (Picture yourself walking into a room with complete self-assurance, unbothered by opinions.)

Day 5: Practicing Small Acts of Confidence

- **Today's Reflection Prompt:**
  "What's one area of my life where I want to feel more confident?"

....

....

- **Today's Affirmation:**
  "I take small steps every day to grow my confidence."

- **Mini-Challenge:**
  Pick one small act of confidence to practice today.
  Example: Make eye contact with people, speak with a louder voice, stand taller, give yourself a compliment.

- **Daily Tracker:**
  | Small Confidence Act Completed ☐ | Affirmation Recited ☐ | Journal Completed ☐ |

- **Meditation Moment:**
  (Picture yourself confidently handling a situation you once avoided.)

Day 6: Weekly Reflection & Milestone Celebration

- **Today's Reflection Prompt:**
  "How has my mindset about confidence shifted this week?"

....

....

- **Today's Affirmation:**
  "I am building unshakable confidence, one step at a time."

- **Milestone Celebration:**
  Write down one limiting belief about confidence you've let go of this week.

  ....

  ....

- **Community Connection (Optional but Encouraged):**
  Who can I share my progress with? _____

Week 1 Summary:

- **One negative belief about confidence I replaced:**

  ....

  ....

  ....

  ....

- **One small act of confidence I practiced this week:**

  ....

  ....

  ....

  ....

- **One way I will continue strengthening my confidence:**

  ....

  ....

  ....

  ....

Preparing for Next Week:

You now understand confidence is a skill you can build.

Next, we'll focus on **body language, communication, and habits that exude confidence and charisma.**

Confidence isn't just a mindset—it's something you express in everything you do. Keep building.

Week 2: Body Language and Presence – Looking the Part (Section 7.2)

Weekly Focus:
Confidence isn't just about **what you say**—it's about **how you carry yourself.**

Your body language **speaks before you do.** The way you stand, move, and make eye contact sends powerful messages about your self-assurance, authority, and presence.

People who exude confidence aren't necessarily the loudest in the room—they're the ones who **own their space, stand tall, and project strength through their actions.**

This week, you'll learn how to:

- Use body language to project confidence, even if you don't feel it yet.
- Develop strong posture, eye contact, and presence that command respect.
- Eliminate habits that make you seem nervous, unsure, or closed off.
- Express confidence nonverbally in conversations, meetings, and social interactions.

Remember:
People believe what your body tells them. Make sure your presence says, "I belong here."

Reginald Dwayne Betts didn't gain confidence overnight—but as he rebuilt his life, he learned that **how he carried himself mattered.** When he walked into Yale Law School, when he stood in court as a lawyer, when he spoke in public—**his presence told a story before he ever said a word.**

This week, you'll do the same by training yourself to **look the part of the confident, capable person you are becoming.**

Day 7: The Power of Posture

- **Today's Reflection Prompt:**
  "How do I carry myself when I feel unsure? How do I stand when I feel confident?"

- **Today's Affirmation:**

  "I stand tall, grounded, and powerful in my presence."

- **Mini-Challenge:**

  Practice "power posing" for 2 minutes today.

  - Stand tall, shoulders back, chest open—just like a leader would.

- **Daily Tracker:**

  | Power Pose Practiced ☐ | Affirmation Recited ☐ | Journal Completed ☐ |

- **Meditation Moment (2–3 min):**

  Visualize yourself standing with confidence in any situation, commanding the room with your presence.

Day 8: Mastering Eye Contact

- **Today's Reflection Prompt:**

  "How comfortable am I with making eye contact? What holds me back?"

- **Today's Affirmation:**

  "I make strong eye contact that shows confidence and respect."

- **Mini-Challenge:**

  Practice making eye contact for 3–5 seconds when speaking to someone today.

- **Daily Tracker:**

  | Eye Contact Practiced ☐ | Affirmation Recited ☐ | Journal Completed ☐ |

- **Meditation Moment:**

  (Picture yourself making effortless, natural eye contact in a conversation.)

Day 9: Eliminating Nervous Habits

- **Today's Reflection Prompt:**
  "What nervous habits do I have that make me look less confident?"

....

....

- **Today's Affirmation:**
  "I am calm, self-assured, and in control of my presence."

- **Mini-Challenge:**
  Identify one nervous habit (fidgeting, crossing arms, avoiding eye contact) and replace it with a confident action.
  Example: Instead of crossing your arms, keep them open and relaxed.

- **Daily Tracker:**
  | Nervous Habit Replaced ☐ | Affirmation Recited ☐ | Journal Completed ☐ |

- **Meditation Moment:**
  (Picture yourself moving with calm, controlled confidence.)

Day 10: Owning the Room – Commanding Presence

- **Today's Reflection Prompt:**
  "How do I feel when I walk into a room full of people? How would I like to feel?"

....

....

- **Today's Affirmation:**
  "I enter every room with confidence and purpose."

- **Mini-Challenge:**
  Walk into a room today with intentional presence—head up, shoulders back, steady pace.

- **Daily Tracker:**
  | Confident Walk Practiced ☐ | Affirmation Recited ☐ | Journal Completed ☐ |

- **Meditation Moment:**
  (Visualize yourself walking into any space radiating self-assurance.)

Day 11: The Confident Handshake and Voice

- **Today's Reflection Prompt:**
  "Does my voice and handshake project confidence? What can I improve?"

....

....

- **Today's Affirmation:**
  "My voice is strong, and my presence is felt."

- **Mini-Challenge:**
  Practice a firm handshake and speak one full sentence with deliberate confidence.

- **Daily Tracker:**
  | Confident Handshake Given ☐ | Affirmation Recited ☐ | Journal Completed ☐ |

- **Meditation Moment:**
  (Picture yourself speaking clearly and shaking hands like a leader.)

Day 12: Weekly Reflection & Milestone Celebration

- **Today's Reflection Prompt:**
  "How has my body language changed this week? How do I feel because of it?"

....

....

- **Today's Affirmation:**
  "I carry myself with confidence in every situation."

- **Milestone Celebration:**
  Write down one body language habit you changed that makes you feel more confident.

....

- **Community Connection (Optional but Encouraged):**
  Who can I share my progress with? _____

Week 2 Summary:

- **One change I made in my body language this week:**

....

....

....

- **One way I feel more confident in my presence:**

....

....

....

- **One body language habit I will continue practicing:**

....

....

....

Preparing for Next Week:

You now understand that confidence isn't just mental—it's physical.

Next, we'll focus on **developing a powerful voice, strong communication skills, and the ability to engage people with ease.**

Confidence isn't just about how you stand—it's about how you speak, connect, and lead.

Week 3: Social Confidence – Owning Any Room You Walk Into (Section 7.3)

Weekly Focus:
Confidence isn't just about how you **feel inside**—it's about how you **present yourself to the world.**

Many people **shrink in social situations** because they fear judgment, rejection, or saying the wrong thing. But the truth is, the most confident people aren't **necessarily the most talented or the most outgoing— they're simply the ones who own their space and energy.**

This week, you'll learn how to:

- Overcome social anxiety and feel comfortable in any environment.
- Make strong first impressions that leave a lasting impact.
- Navigate conversations with ease and confidence.
- Step into leadership roles and command respect in social settings.

Remember:
Owning a room isn't about being the loudest—it's about being the most present, aware, and engaged.

Reginald Dwayne Betts had to **rebuild his confidence in social spaces** after being labeled by his past. Instead of hiding, he learned how to **speak with authority, connect with people, and own every room he entered.**

This week, you'll train yourself to do the same.

Day 13: Mastering the Art of First Impressions

- **Today's Reflection Prompt:**
  "What kind of energy do I bring when I walk into a new space?"

- **Today's Affirmation:**

  "I enter every room with confidence and authenticity."

- **Mini-Challenge:**

  Practice making a strong first impression today—stand tall, smile, and greet someone with presence.

- **Daily Tracker:**

  | Strong First Impression Practiced ☐ | Affirmation Recited ☐ | Journal Completed ☐ |

- **Meditation Moment (2–3 min):**

  Visualize yourself walking into a room and being noticed for your confidence.

Day 14: Eliminating Social Anxiety and Overthinking

- **Today's Reflection Prompt:**

  "Do I second-guess myself in social settings? What triggers it?"

- **Today's Affirmation:**

  "I let go of overthinking and trust myself in social situations."

- **Mini-Challenge:**

  In your next social interaction, focus on listening instead of worrying about what to say next.

- **Daily Tracker:**

  | Social Anxiety Challenge Completed ☐ | Affirmation Recited ☐ | Journal Completed ☐ |

- **Meditation Moment:**

  (Picture yourself feeling completely at ease in a conversation, free from overthinking.)

Day 15: Owning Your Energy in a Room

- **Today's Reflection Prompt:**

  "Do I let other people's energy dictate how I feel in a room?"

- **Today's Affirmation:**

  "I own my energy and set the tone wherever I go."

- **Mini-Challenge:**

  Walk into a public space today and observe how you hold your energy—adjust it to be confident, calm, and open.

- **Daily Tracker:**

  | Energy Ownership Practiced ☐ | Affirmation Recited ☐ | Journal Completed ☐ |

- **Meditation Moment:**

  (Picture yourself walking into a space and bringing calm, confident energy to the environment.)

Day 16: Speaking with Confidence and Clarity

- **Today's Reflection Prompt:**

  "Do I speak with confidence, or do I hold back?"

- **Today's Affirmation:**

  "My words have power, and I speak with clarity and confidence."

- **Mini-Challenge:**

  Have a conversation today where you speak clearly, with a steady voice, and without rushing.

- **Daily Tracker:**

  | Confident Speaking Practiced ☐ | Affirmation Recited ☐ | Journal Completed ☐ |

- **Meditation Moment:**

  (Picture yourself speaking in a group setting, engaging people with ease.)

Day 17: The Charisma Secret – Being Present in Conversations

- **Today's Reflection Prompt:**

  "Do I truly listen when people speak, or do I focus on what to say next?"

....

....

- **Today's Affirmation:**

  "I engage fully in every conversation and connect with people deeply."

- **Mini-Challenge:**

  In your next conversation, put away distractions, make eye contact, and be fully present.

- **Daily Tracker:**

  | Full Engagement in Conversation Practiced ☐ | Affirmation Recited ☐ | Journal Completed ☐ |

- **Meditation Moment:**

  (Picture yourself fully connected in a conversation, making a strong impact on others.)

Day 18: Weekly Reflection & Milestone Celebration

- **Today's Reflection Prompt:**

  "How has my social confidence improved this week?"

....

....

- **Today's Affirmation:**

  "I feel at home in any room I walk into."

- **Milestone Celebration:**

  Write down one way you've become more socially confident this week.

....

....

- **Community Connection (Optional but Encouraged):**

  Who can I share my progress with? _____

Week 3 Summary:

- **One way I've improved my social confidence:**

....

....

....

....

- **One habit I've adopted that makes me more engaging in conversations:**

....

....

....

....

- **One way I will continue strengthening my presence in social settings:**

....

....

....

....

Preparing for Next Week:

You now understand how to own any room and engage people with confidence.

Next, we'll focus on **handling criticism, rejection, and difficult social interactions with unshakable confidence.**

Confidence is not just about looking the part—it's about knowing how to handle any situation with strength and grace.

Week 4: Overcoming Rejection and Criticism with Resilience (Section 7.4)

Weekly Focus:

No matter how confident or successful you become, **you will face rejection, criticism, and judgment.**

The difference between those who **rise to the top** and those who shrink back isn't talent or luck—it's **the ability to handle rejection without letting it destroy their confidence.**

This week, you'll learn how to:

- Develop resilience in the face of rejection and failure.
- Use criticism as a tool for growth, not a source of self-doubt.
- Respond to negative feedback with confidence and emotional control.
- Keep moving forward, no matter what obstacles come your way.

Remember:

Rejection is not a reflection of your worth—it's just part of the process of success.

Reginald Dwayne Betts knows this all too well. After serving time in prison, **he faced judgment at every turn.** People doubted him, criticized him, and tried to define him by his past. But instead of letting rejection break him, **he let it fuel him.**

He became a Yale-educated lawyer, a celebrated poet, and a national advocate—because he refused to let anyone else's opinion dictate his future.

This week, you'll train yourself to **do the same.**

Day 19: Rejection is Redirection

- **Today's Reflection Prompt:**
  "What is one rejection or failure that turned out to be a blessing in disguise?"

....

....

- **Today's Affirmation:**
  "Rejection is not the end—it's a step toward something greater."

- **Mini-Challenge:**
  Write down one rejection or failure you've experienced and find the lesson or opportunity it created.

- **Daily Tracker:**
  | Reframed a Rejection ☐ | Affirmation Recited ☐ | Journal Completed ☐ |

- **Meditation Moment (2–3 min):**
  Visualize rejection as a door closing—but leading you to a better one opening.

Day 20: Separating Self-Worth from Criticism

- **Today's Reflection Prompt:**
  "Do I take criticism personally? How can I separate feedback from my identity?"

- **Today's Affirmation:**
  "I am open to feedback, but I define my own worth."

- **Mini-Challenge:**
  Think about one piece of criticism that has stuck with you. Was it constructive or just someone's opinion? How can you use it for growth instead of self-doubt?

- **Daily Tracker:**
  | Criticism Reframed ☐ | Affirmation Recited ☐ | Journal Completed ☐ |

- **Meditation Moment:**
  (Picture yourself receiving feedback with calmness and confidence, using it only to grow.)

Day 21: Responding to Criticism with Confidence

- **Today's Reflection Prompt:**
  "How do I normally react to criticism? How can I respond with confidence instead?"

....

....

- **Today's Affirmation:**

  "I handle criticism with grace, and I control my reactions."

- **Mini-Challenge:**

  The next time someone criticizes you, pause before reacting and choose to respond with calmness and control.

- **Daily Tracker:**

  | Handled Criticism with Confidence ☐ | Affirmation Recited ☐ | Journal Completed ☐ |

- **Meditation Moment:**

  (Picture yourself receiving negative feedback but staying calm, composed, and confident.)

Day 22: Building Emotional Resilience

- **Today's Reflection Prompt:**

  "When I face failure or rejection, do I give up or push forward?"

....

....

- **Today's Affirmation:**

  "I bounce back stronger from every challenge."

- **Mini-Challenge:**

  Write down one difficult experience where you kept going despite rejection. How did it shape you?

....

....

- **Daily Tracker:**

  | Resilience Exercise Completed ☐ | Affirmation Recited ☐ | Journal Completed ☐ |

- **Meditation Moment:**

  (Picture yourself facing rejection and using it as fuel to move forward with even more confidence.)

Day 23: Turning Failure into Fuel

- **Today's Reflection Prompt:**

  "What would I do if I knew that failure was just part of the process?"

....

....

- **Today's Affirmation:**

  "Failure is not final—it's my stepping stone to success."

- **Mini-Challenge:**

  Take one bold action today that you've been afraid of because of potential failure.

  Example: Apply for a job, start a conversation, share an idea, make a tough decision.

- **Daily Tracker:**

  | Took a Bold Action ☐ | Affirmation Recited ☐ | Journal Completed ☐ |

- **Meditation Moment:**

  (Picture yourself facing a setback but staying strong, knowing it will lead to future success.)

Day 24: Weekly Reflection & Milestone Celebration

- **Today's Reflection Prompt:**

  "How has my mindset about rejection and criticism changed this week?"

....

....

- **Today's Affirmation:**

  "I am unshaken by rejection, and I use it to fuel my growth."

- **Milestone Celebration:**

  Write down one rejection or criticism that no longer affects you the way it used to.

....

....

- **Community Connection (Optional but Encouraged):**

Who can I share my progress with? _____

Week 4 Summary:

- **One way I now handle criticism differently:**

....

....

....

....

- **One rejection I've turned into an opportunity:**

....

....

....

....

- **One way I will continue strengthening my resilience:**

....

....

....

....

Preparing for Next Week:

You now understand that rejection and criticism are just part of the path to success.

Next, we'll focus on **developing true leadership presence, owning your voice, and commanding respect from now on.**

Confidence isn't about avoiding rejection—it's about knowing you can handle anything that comes your way.

Week 5: The Action Plan – Daily Confidence-Building Exercises (Section 7.5)

Weekly Focus:
Confidence isn't just a **mindset**—it's a **habit**.

You've spent the past four weeks strengthening your self-belief, improving your body language, owning social spaces, and learning how to handle rejection. Now, it's time to **solidify these lessons into daily actions that make confidence second nature.**

This final week is about:

- Building consistent confidence-building habits.
- Training yourself to step into every space with self-assurance.
- Creating routines that reinforce self-belief, charisma, and presence.
- Developing unshakable confidence that lasts beyond this 30-day challenge.

Remember:
Confidence isn't something you "achieve" once—it's a muscle you train for life.

Reginald Dwayne Betts didn't just build confidence in his journey from incarceration to success—**he made confidence his way of life.** He knew that every challenge he faced required **the belief that he belonged in every room he walked into.**

Now, it's your turn.

Day 25: Creating Your Personal Confidence Ritual

- **Today's Reflection Prompt:**
  "What actions make me feel the most confident? How can I do them daily?"

....

....

- **Today's Affirmation:**
  "I create daily habits that reinforce my confidence."

- **Mini-Challenge:**
  Design a personal confidence-boosting ritual to start each day with power.
  Example:

  - Power pose for two minutes.

- Repeat a personal mantra.
- Play a song that hypes you up.
- Visualize yourself winning the day.

- **Daily Tracker:**
  | Confidence Ritual Completed ☐ | Affirmation Recited ☐ | Journal Completed ☐ |

- **Meditation Moment (2–3 min):**
  Visualize yourself moving through your day feeling strong, prepared, and confident.

Day 26: Dressing the Part – Confidence Through Appearance

- **Today's Reflection Prompt:**
  "How does the way I dress affect my confidence and how others perceive me?"

....

....

- **Today's Affirmation:**
  "I dress in a way that makes me feel powerful and confident."

- **Mini-Challenge:**
  Choose an outfit today that makes you feel strong, self-assured, and ready to take on anything.

- **Daily Tracker:**
  | Dressed with Confidence ☐ | Affirmation Recited ☐ | Journal Completed ☐ |

- **Meditation Moment:**
  (Picture yourself stepping out into the world with confidence, owning your presence.)

Day 27: Speaking with Confidence – Training Your Voice

- **Today's Reflection Prompt:**
  "Do I speak with certainty, or do I hold back?"

....

....

- **Today's Affirmation:**

"My voice is powerful, and my words matter."

- **Mini-Challenge:**

Practice speaking slowly, clearly, and with purpose in a conversation today.

  - Use a steady tone.

  - Avoid filler words like "uh" or "um."

  - End statements with confidence, not hesitation.

- **Daily Tracker:**

| Spoke with Confidence ☐ | Affirmation Recited ☐ | Journal Completed ☐ |

- **Meditation Moment:**

(Picture yourself speaking to a crowd with complete authority and self-assurance.)

Day 28: Taking Up Space – The Power of Presence

- **Today's Reflection Prompt:**

"Do I shrink myself in social situations, or do I own my space?"

....

....

- **Today's Affirmation:**

"I belong in every room I step into."

- **Mini-Challenge:**

  - **In your next interaction, focus on your body language:**

  - Stand tall.

  - Keep your shoulders open.

  - Make steady eye contact.

  - Own your space with confidence.

- **Daily Tracker:**

| Confident Body Language Practiced ☐ | Affirmation Recited ☐ | Journal Completed ☐ |

- **Meditation Moment:**

(Visualize yourself entering any space with authority, calmness, and confidence.)

Day 29: Taking a Bold Social Risk

- **Today's Reflection Prompt:**
  "What's one thing I've been afraid to do because of self-doubt?"

....

....

- **Today's Affirmation:**
  "I take action despite fear, and confidence grows through my courage."

- **Mini-Challenge:**
  Take one bold social action today.
  Example: Initiate a conversation with a stranger, voice your opinion in a meeting, or post something meaningful online.

- **Daily Tracker:**
  | Bold Action Taken ☐ | Affirmation Recited ☐ | Journal Completed ☐ |

- **Meditation Moment:**
  (Picture yourself fearlessly stepping outside of your comfort zone and owning the moment.)

Day 30: Celebration & Commitment to Lifelong Confidence

- **Today's Reflection Prompt:**
  "How has my confidence transformed over the past 30 days?"

....

....

- **Today's Affirmation:**
  "Confidence is now a part of who I am."

- **Final Mini-Challenge:**
  Write a letter to your future self, reminding yourself of how far you've come and committing to maintaining your confidence. (Space at back of this workbook.)

- **Milestone Celebration:**

  Write down one major way your confidence has improved over the past 30 days.

....

....

- **Community Connection (Optional but Encouraged):**

  Who can I share my progress with? _____

Week 5 Summary: (Final Check-In)

- **One confidence habit I've committed to for life:**

....

....

....

....

- **One way I've changed the way I present myself socially:**

....

....

....

....

- **One bold action I will continue taking moving forward:**

....

....

....

....

You've just completed a **30-day journey in developing unshakable confidence and charisma.** Through mindset shifts, body language mastery, social courage, and resilience, you have trained yourself to **walk into any room, own your space, and handle criticism without shrinking.**

Over the past five weeks, you have:

- Strengthened your belief in yourself and your worth.
- Learned how to use body language and presence to command respect.
- Overcome social fears and developed powerful communication skills.
- Handled rejection and criticism with confidence and emotional control.
- Built daily confidence-building habits that will serve you for life.

But confidence alone isn't enough to create lasting success.

Many people experience **short bursts of confidence, motivation, and success—only to fall back into old patterns when challenges arise.** True transformation happens when confidence and success become **automatic, embedded in your habits and identity.**

That's where Chapter 8 comes in.

Reginald Dwayne Betts didn't just rebuild his confidence once—he **created a life system that ensured his success was sustainable.** He didn't wait for motivation to strike; he built habits and structures that made growth **his default setting.**

In **Chapter 8,** you'll learn how to:

- Make your transformation permanent through identity-based habits.
- Sustain confidence, resilience, and success over the long term.
- Design daily systems that prevent backsliding and self-sabotage.
- Create a lifestyle where personal growth happens effortlessly.

You've built confidence—now let's make success automatic.

Let's begin.

Chapter 8

Making Success Automatic – How to Sustain Your Transformation

Success is not about motivation—it's about consistency. It's about making the right choices so often that they become second nature.

Over the past seven chapters, you've done the hard work of **rewiring your mindset, developing self-discipline, transforming your financial habits, and building unshakable confidence.**

But now comes the most important part—**making sure this transformation lasts.**

Too many people experience breakthroughs **only to fall back into old habits, negative patterns, or self-doubt.** That's because change isn't just about learning new information—it's about **reprogramming your identity and daily habits so success becomes automatic.**

No one understands this better than **Dr. Stanley Andrisse.**

Once labeled a "career criminal," he spent years caught in the justice system. But rather than letting his past dictate his future, **he redefined himself.** Through relentless self-discipline, education, and an unwavering commitment to change, he transformed his identity from an incarcerated man to a **Ph.D. scientist, author, and advocate for formerly incarcerated individuals.**

His success wasn't built on fleeting motivation—it was built on **systems, discipline, and a mindset that refused to accept failure as an option.**

In this final chapter, you'll learn how to:

- Understand why most people relapse into old patterns—and how to avoid it.
- Reprogram your habits and identity for lasting success.
- Create a lifestyle where growth happens automatically.
- Develop a personal system that ensures you never lose momentum.

Success isn't about working harder—it's about making the right choices automatic.

Let's begin by looking at **why so many people fall back into their old ways—and how you can break that cycle for good.**

Week 1: Why Most People Fall Back into Old Patterns (Section 8.1)

Weekly Focus:

Success is easy when you're motivated, focused, and energized. But what happens when:

- **Life gets busy or stressful?**

- **You hit an unexpected obstacle?**

- **Doubt creeps back in, and old habits start calling your name?**

Most people fall back into old patterns **not because they lack discipline—but because they never built systems to make success sustainable.**

This week, you'll learn how to:

- Identify the hidden triggers that pull you back into old behaviors.
- Recognize self-sabotage before it takes over.
- Create habits that make success your default setting.
- Build a lifestyle that protects your progress, even during hard times.

Remember:

If you don't create a system for success, you will unconsciously fall into a system of failure.

Dr. Stanley Andrisse didn't just change his habits—he changed **his identity, environment, and daily systems to make failure impossible.**

This week, you'll take the first step toward doing the same.

Day 1: Recognizing the Triggers That Pull You Back

- **Today's Reflection Prompt:**
  "What situations, emotions, or people tend to make me slip into old patterns?"

....

....

- **Today's Affirmation:**
  "I recognize my triggers and take control of my choices."

- **Mini-Challenge:**

Identify three triggers that have led to setbacks in the past.

Example: Stress → Overeating | Loneliness → Isolating myself | Boredom → Procrastinating.

1. _____

2. _____

3. _____

- **Daily Tracker:**

  | Triggers Identified ☐ | Affirmation Recited ☐ | Journal Completed ☐ |

- **Meditation Moment (2–3 min):**

  Picture yourself recognizing a trigger in real-time and choosing a healthier response.

Day 2: The Self-Sabotage Cycle – Why We Undo Our Progress

- **Today's Reflection Prompt:**

  "Have I ever self-sabotaged my own success? What triggered it?"

....

....

- **Today's Affirmation:**

  "I break the cycle of self-sabotage and embrace lasting success."

- **Mini-Challenge:**

  Write down one past self-sabotaging behavior and one way you will prevent it in the future.

  Example: Procrastinating on opportunities → Set deadlines with accountability.

....

....

- **Daily Tracker:**

  | Self-Sabotage Behavior Addressed ☐ | Affirmation Recited ☐ | Journal Completed ☐ |

- **Meditation Moment:**

  (Visualize yourself making decisions that support your growth instead of holding you back.)

Day 3: Understanding the Power of Identity in Habit Change

- **Today's Reflection Prompt:**

  "Do I see myself as someone who succeeds effortlessly, or do I doubt my own ability to change?"

....

....

- **Today's Affirmation:**

  "I am the type of person who follows through and succeeds."

- **Mini-Challenge:**

  Write a statement that defines your new identity.

  Example: "I am a disciplined person who always follows through."

....

....

- **Daily Tracker:**

  | Identity Shift Statement Created ☐ | Affirmation Recited ☐ | Journal Completed ☐ |

- **Meditation Moment:**

  (Picture yourself fully embodying this new identity every single day.)

Day 4: The Environment Factor – How Your Surroundings Affect Success

- **Today's Reflection Prompt:**

  "Does my environment make success easier or harder for me?"

....

....

- **Today's Affirmation:**

  "I design an environment that supports my success."

- **Mini-Challenge:**

  Make one change to your environment today to support your goals.

  Example: Remove distractions from your workspace, prep healthy meals in advance, or surround yourself with supportive people.

- **Daily Tracker:**

  | Environment Change Made ☐ | Affirmation Recited ☐ | Journal Completed ☐ |

- **Meditation Moment:**

  (Visualize yourself thriving in an environment designed for success.)

Day 5: The Danger of Comfort Zones

- **Today's Reflection Prompt:**

  "What areas of my life am I playing too small? Where am I avoiding discomfort?"

....

....

- **Today's Affirmation:**

  "I embrace discomfort because growth happens outside my comfort zone."

- **Mini-Challenge:**

  Do one thing today that makes you slightly uncomfortable but pushes you toward growth.
  Example: Speak up in a meeting, try a new workout, reach out to someone new.

- **Daily Tracker:**

  | Stepped Outside Comfort Zone ☐ | Affirmation Recited ☐ | Journal Completed ☐ |

- **Meditation Moment:**

  (Picture yourself confidently stepping into discomfort and thriving.)

Day 6: Weekly Reflection & Milestone Celebration

- **Today's Reflection Prompt:**

  "What patterns or triggers have I identified that I will no longer allow to control me?"

....

....

- **Today's Affirmation:**

  "I am in control of my habits, mindset, and future."

- **Milestone Celebration:**

  Write down one old pattern you have broken this week.

- **Community Connection (Optional but Encouraged):**

  Who can I share my progress with? _____

Week 1 Summary:

- **One trigger I identified and overcame:**

....

....

....

....

- **One way I've shifted my identity to match my goals:**

....

....

....

....

- **One habit or behavior I've committed to changing:**

....

....

....

....

Preparing for Next Week:

You now understand why most people fall back into old patterns.

Next, we'll focus on **creating identity-based habits that make your success automatic.**

Transformation isn't about willpower—it's about designing a life that supports your success effortlessly.

Week 2: The Power of Identity-Based Habits (Section 8.2)

Weekly Focus:

Most people try to change by **forcing themselves to act differently,** relying on **willpower** and **motivation** to make new habits stick.

That's why so many **fail**.

Real transformation happens **not when you try to act differently—but when you start to see yourself differently.**

Identity-based habits are the key to lasting change. Instead of saying, "I need to work out," you say, "I am the kind of person who takes care of my body." Instead of saying, "I should start reading more," you say, "I am a person who values knowledge."

Once you **change how you see yourself,** your actions **naturally follow.**

This week, you'll learn how to:

• Rewire your habits by shifting your identity first.
• Replace old, limiting beliefs with new, empowering ones.
• Design systems that make success effortless.
• Create a lifestyle where positive habits feel automatic.

Remember:
You don't rise to the level of your goals—you fall to the level of your identity.

Dr. Stanley Andrisse didn't just change his **habits**—he changed his **identity**. He went from being labeled a **"career criminal"** to becoming a **doctor, author, and leader in criminal justice reform.**

He didn't just say, "I want to succeed." He said, "I am the kind of person who follows through, grows, and wins."

This week, you'll start thinking **the same way.**

Day 7: Who Are You Becoming?

- **Today's Reflection Prompt:**
  "Who do I want to become? What kind of person naturally achieves the success I want?"

....

....

- **Today's Affirmation:**
  "I am becoming the best version of myself, one habit at a time."

- **Mini-Challenge:**
  Write a new identity statement for yourself.
  Example: "I am a leader who takes action daily."

....

....

- **Daily Tracker:**
  | Identity Statement Created ☐ | Affirmation Recited ☐ | Journal Completed ☐ |

- **Meditation Moment (2–3 min):**
  Visualize yourself living fully as this new identity.

Day 8: Linking Habits to Your Identity

- **Today's Reflection Prompt:**
  "What habits do I need to adopt to fully step into my new identity?"

....

....

- **Today's Affirmation:**
  "My habits reflect the person I am becoming."

- **Mini-Challenge:**
  Choose one habit that aligns with your new identity and commit to doing it today.
  Example: If your new identity is "I am a disciplined person," commit to waking up early or following a schedule.

- **Daily Tracker:**
  | Identity-Based Habit Practiced ☐ | Affirmation Recited ☐ | Journal Completed ☐ |

- **Meditation Moment:**
  (Picture yourself performing your new habit easily, without resistance.)

Day 9: Small Wins, Big Momentum

- **Today's Reflection Prompt:**
  "What is one small action I can take daily that will reinforce my new identity?"

....

....

- **Today's Affirmation:**
  "Small consistent actions lead to massive results."

- **Mini-Challenge:**
  Pick a tiny habit and commit to it for the next week.
  Example: Read one page a day, do one push-up, write for five minutes.

- **Daily Tracker:**
  | Small Habit Completed ☐ | Affirmation Recited ☐ | Journal Completed ☐ |

- **Meditation Moment:**
  (Visualize how these small actions will add up over time.)

Day 10: Designing Your Environment for Automatic Success

- **Today's Reflection Prompt:**
  "Does my environment support my new habits, or does it make success harder?"

....

....

- **Today's Affirmation:**
  "I set up my life to make good choices easy and automatic."

- **Mini-Challenge:**

  Change one thing in your environment today that makes your new habit easier.

  Example: Keep a book on your nightstand if you want to read more, prepare healthy snacks if you want to eat better.

- **Daily Tracker:**

  | Environment Change Made ☐ | Affirmation Recited ☐ | Journal Completed ☐ |

- **Meditation Moment:**

  (Picture yourself effortlessly following your habits because your environment supports them.)

Day 11: Eliminating the "Old You" Triggers

- **Today's Reflection Prompt:**

  "What old habits, routines, or relationships pull me back into my past identity?"

....

....

- **Today's Affirmation:**

  "I remove what no longer serves my future."

- **Mini-Challenge:**

  Identify one old habit or trigger that no longer aligns with your goals—and eliminate or replace it today.

  Example: Stop checking social media first thing in the morning, avoid negative conversations.

- **Daily Tracker:**

  | Old Habit Replaced ☐ | Affirmation Recited ☐ | Journal Completed ☐ |

- **Meditation Moment:**

  (Visualize yourself free from old habits that held you back.)

Day 12: Weekly Reflection & Milestone Celebration

- **Today's Reflection Prompt:**

  "How has shifting my identity changed my daily habits this week?"

- **Today's Affirmation:**
  "I am becoming my best self through my daily actions."

- **Milestone Celebration:**
  Write down one identity shift you fully embraced this week.

....

....

- **Community Connection (Optional but Encouraged):**
  Who can I share my progress with? _____

Week 2 Summary:

- **One new identity-based habit I've committed to:**

....

....

....

....

- **One change I made to my environment to support my success:**

....

....

....

....

- **One old habit I've eliminated to become my best self:**

....

....

....

Preparing for Next Week:

You now understand that identity shapes habits—and habits shape your future.

Next, we'll focus on **building an unbreakable system that keeps your success automatic for life.**

When success becomes part of who you are, setbacks can't shake you.

Week 3: Your Personal Success Blueprint (Section 8.3)

Weekly Focus:

Now that you understand **how identity shapes habits,** it's time to create a **concrete, personalized system** that ensures your success is **consistent, automatic, and sustainable.**

Most people fail to maintain their transformation because they **rely on motivation instead of structure.** But when you **build a system for success,** you don't have to wake up every day and "try" to be disciplined—your environment, habits, and mindset **make success effortless.**

You've come too far to leave your success up to chance. Your success blueprint isn't just a plan—it's your promise to yourself that you won't go back. Let's lock it in.

This week, you'll learn how to:

- Create a step-by-step system that reinforces your success.
- Establish routines that keep you growing, even on hard days.
- Track your progress in a way that keeps you motivated.
- Set up accountability structures to ensure long-term consistency.

Remember:
You don't succeed by accident—you succeed by design.

Dr. Stanley Andrisse didn't leave his transformation to chance. He **built a structure** that supported his new habits, goals, and identity. This system kept him moving forward **even when motivation faded, obstacles appeared, and challenges arose.**

This week, you'll design **your own personal blueprint** to make your transformation permanent.

Day 13: Designing Your Daily Non-Negotiables

- **Today's Reflection Prompt:**
  "What small daily actions will keep me aligned with my success?"

....

....

- **Today's Affirmation:**
  "I commit to the habits that make my success inevitable."

- **Mini-Challenge:**
  Identify three daily non-negotiable habits that align with your success goals.
  Example: 10 minutes of reading, morning exercise, journaling.

  1. _____

  2. _____

  3. _____

- **Daily Tracker:**
  | Non-Negotiables Defined ☐ | Affirmation Recited ☐ | Journal Completed ☐ |

- **Meditation Moment (2–3 min):**
  Visualize yourself effortlessly completing your non-negotiables each day.

Day 14: Creating a Weekly Success Check-In

- **Today's Reflection Prompt:**
  "How can I track my progress in a way that keeps me motivated?"

....

....

- **Today's Affirmation:**
  "I review my progress regularly and adjust for continued growth."

....

....

- **Mini-Challenge:**

  Create a weekly check-in ritual to review progress and set new intentions.

  Example: Reflect on wins, lessons, and adjustments needed.

- **Daily Tracker:**

  | Weekly Check-In System Created ☐ | Affirmation Recited ☐ | Journal Completed ☐ |

- **Meditation Moment:**

  (Picture yourself reflecting on your week with clarity, adjusting, and moving forward stronger.)

Day 15: Setting Up Your Accountability System

- **Today's Reflection Prompt:**

  "Who or what will keep me accountable to my goals?"

  ....

  ....

- **Today's Affirmation:**

  "I stay consistent because I have systems and accountability in place."

- **Mini-Challenge:**

  Choose one form of accountability that will keep you consistent.

  Example: Find an accountability partner, use a progress-tracking app, set up a rewards system.

- **Daily Tracker:**

  | Accountability System Established ☐ | Affirmation Recited ☐ | Journal Completed ☐ |

- **Meditation Moment:**

  (Visualize yourself staying committed to your goals because of your accountability system.)

Day 16: Eliminating Decision Fatigue – Automating Your Success

- **Today's Reflection Prompt:**

  "How can I make good choices automatic instead of relying on willpower?"

  ....

- **Today's Affirmation:**

  "I remove obstacles and set myself up for success daily."

- **Mini-Challenge:**

  Automate one aspect of your routine so you don't have to think about it.

  Example: Prep meals in advance, lay out clothes the night before, schedule workouts in advance.

- **Daily Tracker:**

  | Success Automation Implemented ☐ | Affirmation Recited ☐ | Journal Completed ☐ |

- **Meditation Moment:**

  (Picture yourself making good choices automatically because your environment supports them.)

Day 17: Future-Proofing Your Success

- **Today's Reflection Prompt:**

  "What obstacles might threaten my progress? How will I prepare for them?"

- **Today's Affirmation:**

  "I anticipate challenges and create solutions before they arise."

- **Mini-Challenge:**

  Identify three potential obstacles and write a solution for each.

  Example: If I lose motivation → I will re-read my goals and listen to a podcast that inspires me.

  1. _____

  2. _____

  3. _____

- **Daily Tracker:**

  | Future Challenges Planned For ☐ | Affirmation Recited ☐ | Journal Completed ☐ |

- **Meditation Moment:**

(Picture yourself handling future challenges with ease and confidence.)

Day 18: Weekly Reflection & Milestone Celebration

- **Today's Reflection Prompt:**
  "How has building a success system made my progress easier?"

....

....

- **Today's Affirmation:**
  "My system ensures that my success is sustainable."

- **Milestone Celebration:**
  Write down one key success system you've put in place this week.

....

....

- **Community Connection (Optional but Encouraged):**
  Who can I share my progress with? _____

Week 3 Summary:

- **One daily habit I've made non-negotiable:**

....

....

....

....

- **One accountability system that will keep me consistent:**

....

....

....

....

- **One challenge I've prepared for in advance:**

....

....

....

....

Preparing for Next Week:

You now have a personalized system that makes success sustainable.

Next, we'll focus on **refining this system so that your transformation lasts for years—not just months.**

The more effortless success feels, the more unstoppable you become.

Week 4: Accountability & Continuous Growth (Section 8.4)

Weekly Focus:

Success is **not a one-time achievement**—it's an ongoing process of growth, reflection, and refinement.

The most successful people don't just set goals and forget about them. They:

- **Track their progress** to stay on course.
- **Have accountability systems** that keep them committed.
- **Keep learning and growing** instead of becoming complacent.

If you don't create **accountability structures,** it's easy to slip back into old patterns. But when you build a system that **keeps you engaged and growing,** your success will continue for life.

This week, you'll learn how to:

- Build an accountability system that keeps you on track.
- Reflect on progress and make necessary adjustments.
- Surround yourself with people who push you to grow.
- Maintain long-term personal and professional development.

Remember:

Growth never stops—unless you stop pushing yourself.

Dr. Stanley Andrisse didn't stop once he earned his Ph.D. He continued growing, mentoring others, and building his legacy. **Success wasn't just an achievement—it became his way of life.**

This week, you'll do the same.

Day 19: Setting Up a Personal Accountability System

- **Today's Reflection Prompt:**
  "What will keep me accountable when motivation fades?"

....

....

- **Today's Affirmation:**
  "I stay committed to my success by holding myself accountable."

- **Mini-Challenge:**
  Choose an accountability system that will help you stay consistent.
  Example: A weekly check-in with a mentor, a journal for tracking progress, a habit-tracking app.

- **Daily Tracker:**
  | Accountability System Set Up ☐ | Affirmation Recited ☐ | Journal Completed ☐ |

- **Meditation Moment (2–3 min):**
  Visualize yourself checking in on your progress regularly and feeling proud of your consistency.

Day 20: Reviewing & Adjusting Your Progress

- **Today's Reflection Prompt:**
  "What's working well in my success journey? What needs improvement?"

....

....

- **Today's Affirmation:**
  "I review my progress with honesty and make necessary adjustments."

- **Mini-Challenge:**

  Write down one success habit you'll keep and one area you'll improve.

  ....

  ....

- **Daily Tracker:**

  | Progress Review Completed ☐ | Affirmation Recited ☐ | Journal Completed ☐ |

- **Meditation Moment:**

  (Picture yourself refining your habits and improving every day.)

Day 21: Surrounding Yourself with Growth-Minded People

- **Today's Reflection Prompt:**

  "Do the people around me push me forward or hold me back?"

  ....

  ....

- **Today's Affirmation:**

  "I attract and surround myself with people who inspire growth."

- **Mini-Challenge:**

  Identify one person or community that aligns with your goals and find a way to engage with them. Example: A mastermind group, a networking event, a mentorship opportunity.

  ....

  ....

- **Daily Tracker:**

  | Growth-Oriented Connection Made ☐ | Affirmation Recited ☐ | Journal Completed ☐ |

- **Meditation Moment:**

  (Picture yourself surrounded by people who uplift, challenge, and support your growth.)

Day 22: The Power of Teaching & Mentoring

- **Today's Reflection Prompt:**
  "Who can I help by sharing what I've learned on my journey?"

....

....

- **Today's Affirmation:**
  "I strengthen my own growth by helping others grow."

- **Mini-Challenge:**
  Teach or mentor one person today—share advice, a resource, or encouragement.

- **Daily Tracker:**
  | Mentorship or Guidance Given ☐ | Affirmation Recited ☐ | Journal Completed ☐ |

- **Meditation Moment:**
  (Visualize yourself as a mentor, guiding someone else toward success.)

Day 23: Lifelong Learning – Staying Ahead of the Curve

- **Today's Reflection Prompt:**
  "How can I keep learning and evolving so I never become stagnant?"

....

....

- **Today's Affirmation:**
  "I am committed to lifelong learning and continuous improvement."

- **Mini-Challenge:**
  Choose one resource (book, podcast, online course) that will challenge you to grow and commit to it.

- **Daily Tracker:**
  | Lifelong Learning Resource Selected ☐ | Affirmation Recited ☐ | Journal Completed ☐ |

- **Meditation Moment:**
  (Picture yourself constantly evolving, gaining knowledge, and becoming wiser every year.)

Day 24: Weekly Reflection & Milestone Celebration

- **Today's Reflection Prompt:**
  "What changes have I made that are now part of my identity?"

....

....

- **Today's Affirmation:**
  "I am always growing, improving, and pushing myself to new heights."

- **Milestone Celebration:**
  Write down one major way you have grown over the past month.

....

....

- **Community Connection (Optional but Encouraged):**
  Who can I share my progress with? _____

Week 4 Summary:

- **One accountability habit I've established:**

....

....

....

....

- **One area of growth I will continue working on:**

....

....

....

....

- **One way I will push myself to keep learning and evolving:**

....

....

....

....

Preparing for Next Week:

You now have an accountability system that ensures long-term success.

Next, we'll focus on **finalizing your personal transformation plan—so success remains effortless for life.**

When you commit to growth as a lifestyle, success is inevitable.

Week 5: Locking in Your New Life (Section 8.5)

Weekly Focus:

You've come a long way.

You've transformed your mindset, built unshakable confidence, created powerful habits, and designed a system for lasting success. Now, the final step is to **solidify your transformation so you never fall back into old patterns.**

This last week is about:

- Ensuring your new habits and mindset become permanent.
- Developing a strategy for handling future challenges.
- Creating a personal success contract to hold yourself accountable.
- Locking in your new identity so success becomes second nature.

Remember:

This is no longer a temporary change—this is who you are now.

Dr. Stanley Andrisse didn't just escape his past—he **rewrote his future.** He didn't rely on willpower or luck; he built a **lifestyle that made growth and success automatic.**

Now, you are doing the same.

Day 25: Reviewing Your Journey – How Far You've Come

- **Today's Reflection Prompt:**
  "What are the biggest changes I've made in my mindset and habits?"

....

....

- **Today's Affirmation:**
  "I acknowledge my growth and fully step into my new identity."

- **Mini-Challenge:**
  Write down three major transformations you've made since starting this journey.

....

....

- **Daily Tracker:**
  | Transformation Reflected On ☐ | Affirmation Recited ☐ | Journal Completed ☐ |

- **Meditation Moment (2–3 min):**
  Visualize your past self and your current self—see the growth, the resilience, the transformation.

Day 26: Defining Your Non-Negotiables for Life

- **Today's Reflection Prompt:**
  "What habits, standards, and beliefs will I never compromise on again?"

....

....

- **Today's Affirmation:**
  "I set clear non-negotiables that define my new life."

- **Mini-Challenge:**

  List five non-negotiables that will guide your decisions moving forward.

  Example: I will always prioritize my growth. I will never lower my standards for toxic relationships.

  ....

  ....

  ....

  ....

  ....

- **Daily Tracker:**

  | Non-Negotiables Defined ☐ | Affirmation Recited ☐ | Journal Completed ☐ |

- **Meditation Moment:**

  (Picture yourself living in full alignment with your non-negotiables.)

Day 27: Preparing for Future Challenges

- **Today's Reflection Prompt:**

  "What obstacles might try to pull me back into old habits? How will I handle them?"

  ....

  ....

- **Today's Affirmation:**

  "I am prepared for any challenge that comes my way."

- **Mini-Challenge:**

  Create a "Challenge Response Plan"—write down potential setbacks and how you will overcome them.

  ....

  ....

- **Daily Tracker:**

  | Challenge Plan Created ☐ | Affirmation Recited ☐ | Journal Completed ☐ |

- **Meditation Moment:**
  (Visualize yourself handling a challenge with strength and confidence.)

Day 28: Writing Your Personal Success Contract

- **Today's Reflection Prompt:**
  "What commitment am I making to myself for life?"

....

....

- **Today's Affirmation:**
  "I hold myself accountable to my highest potential."

- **Mini-Challenge:**
  Write and sign a personal success contract stating your commitment to your new life.

- **Daily Tracker:**
  | Success Contract Written & Signed ☐ | Affirmation Recited ☐ | Journal Completed ☐ |

- **Meditation Moment:**
  (Feel the power of committing to yourself and your future.)

Day 29: Your Vision for the Future

- **Today's Reflection Prompt:**
  "What does my future look like if I stay consistent with my transformation?"

....

....

- **Today's Affirmation:**
  "I am creating a future filled with success, purpose, and growth."

- **Mini-Challenge:**
  Write a vision statement describing your life five years from now.

....

....

....

....

- **Daily Tracker:**
  | Future Vision Written ☐ | Affirmation Recited ☐ | Journal Completed ☐ |

- **Meditation Moment:**
  (Picture your future self thriving, fulfilled, and fully in alignment with your purpose.)

Day 30: Celebration & Stepping into Your New Identity

- **Today's Reflection Prompt:**
  "What does it feel like to be fully in control of my future?"

....

....

- **Today's Affirmation:**
  "This is my life now—I am successful, disciplined, and unstoppable."

- **Final Mini-Challenge:**
  Write a letter to your past self, sharing the wisdom and strength you have gained. (Space at back of this workbook.)

- **Milestone Celebration:**
  Write down one final breakthrough you've experienced.

....

....

- **Community Connection (Optional but Encouraged):**
  Who can I share my success with? _____

Final Week Summary:

- **One powerful realization I've had about myself:**

....

....

....

....

- **One non-negotiable I will always live by:**

....

....

....

....

- **One way I will ensure my success remains permanent:**

....

....

....

....

You didn't just complete another self-help book—you rewired your entire way of thinking.

Through discipline, consistency, and relentless commitment, you have **broken free from the cycles that once held you back.** You now understand that success isn't something that happens to other people—it's something you create, something you control, and something you sustain.

Over the past 30 days, you have:

- Transformed your mindset and built resilience.
- Replaced self-sabotage with identity-based habits.
- Designed a personal success blueprint that keeps you growing for life.
- Committed to accountability, lifelong learning, and continuous growth.

But most importantly, **you have proven to yourself** that you are capable of lasting change.

Dr. Stanley Andrisse didn't let his past define him—**he chose his future.** And now, **you are doing the same.**

The question is no longer "Can I change?" because you already have.

Now the only question is:

What will you do with your new life?

Final Words

Your Journey is Just Beginning

You've done what most people only dream about—you've **taken full control of your life.**

Most individuals who have faced hardship never make it to this point. They stay stuck, believing the lie that they can never change. But you? You refused to accept that. **You showed up, you put in the work, and you proved to yourself that you are greater than your past.**

You now carry with you **the mindset, the habits, and the confidence to walk into any room, face any challenge, and build the life you deserve.**

No more playing small. No more second-guessing yourself. No more falling back into old cycles.

From here on out, you are a **leader**—not just in your own life, but for others who need to see what's possible. Your transformation doesn't just impact you—it **creates a ripple effect.**

And that's why I can't wait to see what you accomplish next.

This is not the end of your journey.

This is just the beginning.

Go build your legacy. I'll be cheering for you every step of the way. -Jackie

Letter to my Future Self

Throughout this journey of rebuilding your life, you'll confront powerful emotions, uncover deep truths, and reclaim the strength that may have been hidden beneath layers of hardship. Writing a letter to your future self is a powerful act—an opportunity to envision your life transformed by resilience, clarity, and purpose. This isn't simply an exercise in imagination; it's an act of intention, a declaration of your commitment to breaking free from old cycles.

....

....

....

....

....

....

....

....

....

....

....

....

Chapter 1-Notes

Day 30: Letter to my Future Self

Final Mini-Challenge:

Write a letter to your future self, describing what you've learned, how you feel, and your commitment to staying on this path.

....

....

....

....

....

....

....

....

....

....

....

....

....

....

Day 30: Letter to my Future Self

Final Mini-Challenge:

Write a letter to your future self, describing what you've learned, how you feel, and your commitment to your new path..

....

....

....

....

....

....

....

....

....

....

....

....

....

....

Day 30: Letter to my Future Self

Final Mini-Challenge:

Write a letter to your future self, describing what you've learned, how you feel, and your commitment to facing fear daily.

....

....

....

....

....

....

....

....

....

....

....

....

....

....

Day 30: Letter to my Future Self

Final Mini-Challenge:

Write a letter to your future self about your transformation and commitment to protecting your peace.

....

....

....

....

....

....

....

....

....

....

....

....

....

Chapter 5-Notes

Day 30: Letter to my Future Self

Final Mini-Challenge:
Write a letter to your future self, committing to maintaining your self-discipline for life.

....

....

....

....

....

....

....

....

....

....

....

....

....

Day 30: Letter to my Future Self

Final Mini-Challenge:

Write a letter to your future self, committing to maintaining your wealth-building habits for life.

....

....

....

....

....

....

....

....

....

....

....

....

....

....

Day 30: Letter to my Future Self

Final Mini-Challenge:

Write a letter to your future self, reminding yourself of how far you've come and committing to maintaining your confidence.

....

....

....

....

....

....

....

....

....

....

....

....

....

....

Day 30: Letter to my Future Self

Final Mini-Challenge:

Write a letter to your past self, sharing the wisdom and strength you have gained.

....

....

....

....

....

....

....

....

....

....

....

....

....

www.ingramcontent.com/pod-product-compliance
Lightning Source LLC
Chambersburg PA
CBHW081532120626
46550CB00009B/2698